**A FINE LINE
BETWEEN
OBLIVIOUS
AND INANITY**

Copyright © David Thorne 2021 All rights reserved.

ISBN 978-1-7353286-1-4 DWFC 288M07
A Fine Line Between Oblivious and Inanity

www.27bslash6.com

This book is sold subject to the condition that it shall not, by way of trade or otherwise, be lent, re-sold, hired out, re-produced on the Internet or otherwise circulated without the author's prior consent in any form of binding or cover other than that in which it is published. Activities and vehicle modifications appearing or described in this book may be potentially dangerous.

By the same author:

The Internet is a Playground
The *New York Times* bestselling first release by David Thorne featuring articles from 27bslash6 plus over 160 pages of new material.

I'll Go Home Then; It's Warm and Has Chairs
The second collection of all new essays and emails.

Look Evelyn, Duck Dynasty Wiper Blades, We Should Get Them
The third collection of new essays and emails.

That's Not How You Wash a Squirrel
The fourth collection of new essays and emails.

Wrap It In a Bit of Cheese Like You're Tricking the Dog
The fifth collection of new essays and emails.

Walk It Off, Princess
The sixth collection of new essays and emails.

Burning Bridges to Light the Way
The seventh collection of all new essays and emails.

Sixteen Different Flavours of Hell
The eighth collection of all new essays and emails.

OFFICE MEMO PRESS

Not for sale outside of Australia

Alternate Titles for This Book

Free Eyepads With Every Copy

A Brief History of Clogs

Snippets

Corridor Dog

How to Make Your Own Bags of Sand

Wait, I've Read This One Before

No Refunds

All Profits Go Towards Bitcoin

Who Edited This?

Scope Reactor 3000

There's Nothing In Here About Pufferfish

Ropey Ropey Rope Rope

Grandma's Here. Everyone Cheer.

Book

Reviews

"Writing 350 on the last page doesn't make it 350 pages."

Steve Nagy

"It's kind of like Scrabble but with words."

Korneel Bullens

"The part about Germans having no sense of humour simply isn't true. I know 48 jokes about knees."

Philip Schüller

"Thanks for the rubber snake."

Michael Reed

"I counted 432 spelling errors. They were the best part of the book."

Kelsie Shanks

"I'm getting married at the end of May. Please don't mention anywhere in the book that I had an affair with an electrician named Roger.

Sammi Wootton

Contents

Foreword 15
Dana Plato 17
Elk's Lodge 20
Stroke 21
Knots 23
Mr Mercury 24
Shipping Labels 25
Commercials 26
Paddleboards 27
Love Gun 28
BYO Chairs 29
Smoke 30
Fire 31
Texting 32
Immigration 33
Cats 34
Mugs 35
Pet Names 37
Backrubs 38
Rocket Bike 39
Survival 41
Toasted Sandwiches 45
Seattle Real Estate 46
Beaches 47

Rabies	48
Tiny Houses	49
Charades	50
Facebook	51
Spring Onions	53
Tractors	54
Windows	59
Goth	60
Schewel's	61
Staff Retreat	62
Falling Water	63
Pool Float	65
Badminton	66
Cheese	73
Pumpkins	74
Art Students	77
Eskimo Day	78
Nacho Soup	79
Japanese Porn	81
Yemen	82
Trapdoor	83
Romance	99
Love is Love	100
Relationships	101
Fast Clowns	102
Medieval Society	103
Girls Named Louise	104
Wills	105
Fondue	106

Coloured Things	107
Scriptwriters	111
Didits	112
Monkey-Bar Intel	115
Bin	116
Mammoths	117
Baby Birds	119
Alpha-Crotinials	123
Ben's Shirt	124
Hedgehogs	125
HOA	129
Jason Statham	131
TJ Maxx	135
The Recipient Incident	136
Kombucha	137
Paintball	139
Blink 182	143
Thanksgiving	144
Ace Frehley	145
Part of the Family	147
Blisters	151
Cocksucker	153
Dancing	154
Pineapple	155
St. Judes	156
Bed Bath & Beyond	157
Baby Carrot	158
Number Plate People	159
Naps	179

Helmets	180
The Meadows	181
Socks	187
Poetry	188
Tampa	189
Hiking	192
Exercise	195
Xanadu	197
Pickle	198
Baths	201
Runaway	202
Fences	203
Algorithms	204
Chores	205
Doubling Down	207
French	208
Stains	209
Cargo Shorts	215
Maps	216
Mr Steve	217
AT&T	218
Man Cave	219
Greenpeace	223
Vaping	224
Blue Eyeshadow	225
Method Acting	229
Gossip	230
Seven Seconds	231
Lawn	233

Television	234
Karaoke	237
Locks	241
Rednecks	242
Fat Dog	243
Judgmental	242
Sorry Bradley Died	247
Listening Skills	248
The Spot	249

Foreword

"Gosh. A new book out already, David? That was quick."
"Yes, I suppose it was."
"You must have been very busy. Your last book came out, what, three weeks ago?"
""Several weeks actually. What are you implying?"
"Nothing."
"I'm quite prolific."
"Yes, you must be to write 350 pages of new content in that time frame. It is all new isn't it?"
"Newish."
"Oh my god. It's not just all your old stuff again is it?"
"It's best to think of it as snippets."
"Snippets?"
"Yes. Snippets from books that were either not sold in Australia or contained edited content at the time."
"You really have no shame, do you?"
"I make up for it in other ways."
"You do?"
"Yes, people have told me I'm rather personable."
"What people?"
"You don't know them. They live in Canada."

Dana Plato

When I was young, complaining about what you were given for dinner would result in an immediate suspension of television privileges for the evening - which might not seem too harsh but my father's version included a chair next to the television that you had to sit on and watch the rest of the family watching television from. If you tilted forward and turned your head towards the television, he'd aim the remote control towards you and yell, "Pause." Three 'pauses' and you were 'off' which meant sitting in the chair with a tea towel over your head.

"Wow, you're certainly missing an exciting episode tonight, David. It isn't a holiday resort planet after all, it's a trap set by the Cylons. Starbuck and Apollo are walking straight into it. Perhaps you'll think about that the next time you decide to comment on how lumpy the Gravox® is."

For those not familiar with Gravox®, it's a waterproof brown gravy-flavoured powder to which you add water and stir. When you poke at the resulting lumps, they burst and produce clouds of dust like the slow-motion videos you see of mushrooms shooting spores. My mother cut her thumb quite badly on the inside edge of a tin of Gravox® one day and required several stitches. She wrote a lengthy letter to the company informing them of the mishap and a few weeks later, a truck delivered two pallets containing hundreds of tins of the horrible stuff.

To my father, it was like winning the lottery and practically every evening meal for the next few years was smothered in it. I missed a lot of television during that time.

"Did you watch *Knight Rider* last night?"
"Um... yes."
"Best episode ever. What was your favourite part?"
"The bit where the car talked."
"Kitt talks in every episode."
"I know, right? How awesome would it be to have a talking car?"
"My favourite part was when the bridge was out but Michael pushed the turbo button at the last minute and Kitt flew over it."
"Yeah, that was pretty good. The car should be able to press its own turbo button though."
"What?"
"If the car can talk and do all sorts of other things, it should be able to press its own turbo button when it needs to."
"Then you wouldn't need Michael."
"Apart from pressing the turbo button, the car can drive itself so it doesn't really need Michael anyway. I don't know why Michael doesn't just stretch out in the passenger seat. Or lie down in the back."
"It's his car, he can sit where he wants. Besides, if he was in

the back he'd have to reach all the way over to press the turbo button. Did you watch *Diff'rent Strokes?*"

"Um... yes."

"If I was Willis, I'd fuck Kimberley. She's not his real sister. Do you sometimes wish you could jump into a girl's body, like take over her mind, and then go to your house and knock on the door and when you answer say, 'It's me, I'm in this girl's body. Quick, lets have sex?'"

"Um... no."

"No, I don't either. I was just asking if you do."

Interestingly, Dana Plato, the girl who played Kimberly, didn't have much of an acting career after *Diff'rent Strokes*. She posed for *Playboy* and worked at a dry-cleaners before trying her hand at armed robbery. On February 28, 1991, she entered a video store, produced a gun, and demanded money from the register. The clerk called 911 saying, "I've just been robbed by the girl who played Kimberly on *Diff'rent Strokes*."

I'm not making this up. She died of a drug overdose a few years later in a Winnebago. The guy who played Willis defeated Vanilla Ice on an episode of *Celebrity Boxing* a few years back so he's doing pretty well for himself. The little black kid and the dad are dead.

Elk's Lodge

My friend JM invited me to a Elk's Lodge meeting last year. I was quite excited but it turned out to be just a bunch of old men in ill-fitting suits standing in a room eating luncheon meats and sharing hip-surgery updates.

One of the old men gave me a lengthy account of his trip to Target to buy a toaster and another scolded me for being Australian. Apparently he knew an Australian named Bill during the war, possibly the Civil War, who stole his watch. It was a watch that his father had given him that his father's father had given his father... I phased out after five minutes but from what I could tell, the watch had been handed down since sometime during the Mesozoic period. Not having Bill's side of the story, I suggested that the watch may have been lost and was met with a slammed down plate of luncheon meats and the yelled rebuttal, "It was on a chain!"

After everyone had finished their luncheon meats, they led a naked young man wearing an elk mask into the middle of the room, formed a circle around him, and took turns giving him their seed. I left before the ritual but I'm pretty sure that's what happens. I didn't go to any more meetings because JM told me that once a year, members have to go door-to-door selling brooms for deaf kids or something.

Stroke

I know a guy named Jason that used to work as an EMT and he told me that a surprisingly large amount of people die on the toilet. Apparently pushing out a big poo puts the cardiovascular system at risk by raising blood pressure, increasing the risk of a stroke or heart attack. I'm at that age where I can have a stroke or drop dead at any time so I always make sure my hair looks good and I'm wearing clean underwear before I take a dump. I also cover my genitals with a towel and make sure my browser history has been deleted.

My Uncle Keith had paralysis on the left side of his face from a stroke and it wasn't pleasant to look at. The half that wasn't paralyzed was pretty dreadful to look at too though, so it's not as if his stroke meant the loss of any potential modeling contracts. If anything, the paralyzed side looked better; like it was just hanging out relaxed, maybe sleeping.

To make up for the loss of expression, Uncle Keith over-emphasized his 'good side' expressions like a coked-up ventriloquist dummy. Slight smiles were terrifying grins, a raised eyebrow looked like he was riding in one of those spinning things that astronauts train in, and a mildly cross look looked like he was straining to push out the world's largest poo. Sometimes I'd hold up my hand so I could only see the paralyzed side of his face while he was talking to me. He didn't like that much and would take his poo straining expression to new levels.

Uncle Keith had a second stroke a few years after the first, it balanced things out a bit, but his third stroke killed him. He died in an airplane toilet during a flight from Adelaide to Sydney, which is only worth mentioning as it supports the early statement about making sure your hair looks nice and deleting your browser history before taking a dump.

Knots

I grew up around boats. My grandfather regularly took me fishing on his wooden skiff when I was young. Sometimes he'd let me drive and he taught me how to dock; as we approached a pier, I'd jump off the boat and my grandfather would throw me a rope to loop around a pillar. Sometimes I'd miss the rope and he'd yell, "You wee useless cunt!" He wasn't Scottish, just a dick.

He also showed me how to tie several knots but I've forgotten them all now. I usually just use ratchet straps anyway. If I do have to tie a knot, I just tie several granny knots over the top of each other and figure they'll squeeze together to form the world's best knot.

"Is this rope tangled?"
"No, Holly, that's a sailor's knot. A Sheep's Hitch Double Shot knot."
"Did you just make that up?"
"No."
"It sounds made up."
"Well it's not. My grandfather taught me it."
"How do I get it undone?"
"Ah, there's a bit of a trick to it. You'll need a pair of needle nosed pliers or a sharp knife."

Mr Mercury

One of my teachers at school was named Mr Mercury. He was a huge fan of the band Queen and, sharing the last name of the group's lead singer, loved it when people asked if he was related to Freddie. He said he was, and that Freddie had been to his house several times, but I've learnt since that Freddie Mercury's real name was Farrokh Bulsara so I call bullshit.

Mr Mercury also told us that he could hold his breath underwater for three minutes but who can trust anything he claimed? I saw him at a basketball game years later and I thought about saying something but he was a couple of seats down and several across and he'd lost a hand somehow. He had one of those beige attachments with a stainless steel claw and pulleys.

I know a guy named Jeff who also has a claw hand. I asked him once if it gives him an advantage when he plays the claw machines at arcades and he replied, "I've never played one but probably."

My friend Ross is excellent at them but he doesn't have a claw hand, he's just semi-autistic and practices at home with a Lego Technic crane.

Shipping Labels

I once ordered a set of 'Japanese Garden Lanterns' online that had the description, "A centuries-old art form, these traditional Japanese lanterns are sure to take pride of place in any garden or patio setting." I received a foot-long string of lights, powered by a single AAA battery, with four plastic lanterns each an inch in diameter. There were meant to be five lanterns but one of the LEDs was missing one. I doubt very much that Japanese people living centuries ago invited guests out to their garden to show off their foot long string of plastic lanterns.

"They're beautiful Mr Yamaha, but is that LED missing a lantern?"
"Yes, I should probably wrap a bit of electrical tape around that LED so it isn't so obvious."

I wrapped a bit of electrical tape around the bare LED so it wasn't so obvious and hung the string of lanterns outside on a branch. It wasn't long enough to reach another branch so it hung vertically. Rather than adding a touch of the exotic to my outdoor lifestyle, it added a fair degree of disappointment. After a few days, I hid it in a kitchen drawer. I should probably have returned it but that would have entailed printing out a shipping label.

Commercials

There are a lot of commercials for pharmaceutical drugs on American television. Watching an episode of *Jeopardy* will subject you to at least twenty different advertisements featuring old people finally able to push their grandkids on a swing thanks to Ethdytrin or Apibatipopyol. There's so many drug brands that the marketing teams have given up bothering to come up with clever names and adopted the Scrabble bag shake, dump, and run with it approach.

"What's this drug do?"
"It stops dry eyes by reprogramming the part of the brain that controls the tear ducts."
"Any side effects?"
"Some people reported depression, loss of vision, paralysis and death, but we'll mention that soothingly in the commercial."
"Good. What are we going to call it?"
"Well, we were thinking Fsdfwjffdghrte. Keith came up with it when he had a stroke while typing. He's on medication that thins nose hairs."

Paddleboards

I've no idea why paddleboarding is a thing. Nobody cares that you have good balance; it's essentially the same skill as standing on a wobbly stool. The person who invented paddleboarding, probably someone who wears a lot of Prana, should have been told to stop fucking about and sit down.

"Stop fucking about and sit down. You'll hurt yourself."
"No I won't, I have really good balance."
"Nobody cares. What's the point?"
"The point is that I'm standing up. Look at me!"
"You don't look very stable."
"I'm not."
"Or comfortable."
"No."
"You'd be better off in a kayak. They have a seat and a paddle with blades on both ends so you can row faster."
"It's not about speed. It's about standing up. I'm going to call it the Stand Up and Paddle Board."
"So it's just a water version of your other inventions, the Stand Up and Drive Car, the Stand Up and Sleep Bed, and the Stand Up and Wobble Stool?"
"Yes, but I have good feeling about this one."
"That's what you said about the Stand Up and Defecate Toilet and the Stand Up and Roll Wheelchair."

Love Gun

My sister once had a boyfriend named Trevor. He had long curly hair and owned a metallic blue panel-van with the members of the band KISS painted on the side.

Trevor also had one leg shorter than the other and had a special shoe with a three-inch heel. He enjoyed giving me dead arms so one day I did a poo in a plastic bag and wiped it into the air vents of his car.

Trevor died in a car crash a few months later. Not because of the poo, apparently he was low on fuel so switched the car off to coast down a big hill. At the bottom, he tried to turn and the steering lock engaged. He went through the front window of a H&R Block and was decapitated by a giant green square.

I caught the bus with my sister to his funeral. They played *Love Gun*.

BYO Chairs

How good can a barbecue be if the host can't organize chairs? I'll stay at home with my vast selection of things to sit on if you can't get your act together. I specifically tell people not to bring their own chairs when I have a barbecue. I paid a lot of money for our outdoor setting and I don't want anyone's shitty Coleman fold-up camping chairs ruining the layout. Not enough chairs? Stand. No, we're not bringing the dining room chairs outside, they're West Elm.

"David, I'm having a barbecue tomorrow if you're free. I'll fire up the grill around noon."
"Do I have to bring anything?"
"No, just a chair."
"Are you having the barbecue in a field?"
"No, it's at my house but apparently we don't own chairs. Oh, and it's BYO so bring something to drink and whatever you want put on the grill. And a side dish."
"So pack as if I'm going camping, got it. Will anything actually be provided?"
"The venue and great company."
"Right, I'll probably just stay home then."
"No, you have to come. I need you to pick up six bags of ice and a full propane bottle on the way. And a patio umbrella from Home Depot, it's going to be sunny."

Smoke

Both my parents smoked when I was young. They smoked in the house, they smoked while playing tennis, and they smoked in the car.

"Why are you coughing? You'd better not be getting sick."
"It's smoky in here. Can I wind down my window?"
"No, the air conditioner is on. I don't know what you're carrying on about, your mother and I are the ones smoking and we're not coughing."
"Just a little bit? I can't breathe."
"Fine. Just half an inch though. You can stick your drinking straw through the gap and breathe through that if you are going to be a dickhead about it."
"How long before we get there?"
"Four or five hours. It depends on the traffic."

My father gave up smoking a few years later and became one of those annoying ex-smokers. My mother still smoked so my father kept a can of air-freshener in the car. Once he sprayed her hair.

Fire

There was a fire in the office kitchen this morning. It started in a toaster oven and lit the shelf above. It wasn't a very big fire and didn't cause a lot of damage but it was still quite exciting at the time; there was screaming and yelling and people trying to work out how to use the fire extinguisher. It hadn't been checked since August 1986 according to the label and made only a small 'pthh' sound when the trigger was pulled. It was Ben who eventually smothered the fire, with a wet tea towel, and he was quite proud of the fact.

"It probably would have set the entire building on fire if I hadn't managed to put it out."
"Yes, you're very brave, Ben. Like a tiny, shaved version of Smokey Bear. Tell us the story again."
"I didn't see you rushing to put it out."
"Only you can prevent office fires. Besides, you seemed to know what you were doing. I particularly liked the bit where you threw the fire extinguisher at it. Very effective. Now we have to replace the toaster *and* the microwave."
"You can't handle anyone else being the hero can you? Not everything has to be about you, David."
"Please. Who do you think is going to be remembered for the kitchen fire - the person who put it out or the person who started it?"

Texting

I've never understood why people text while driving. It's like playing the game Operation while riding a horse. My partner Holly texts me while she's driving all the time and, when I admonish her for it, she declares, "I'm capable of doing more than one thing at a time." Which is true of most people but it's hardly going to stand up as a viable justification in court.

"If I understand this correctly, Mrs Thorne, you were playing Twister, reading a book, and changing your pants when you drove through a school crossing and killed fifteen children. Do you have anything to say in your defence?"
"I'm capable of doing more than one thing at a time."
"Yes, most people are. Excellent point. Case dismissed."

I won't even answer calls when I'm driving let alone read and reply to text messages.

"I rang you thirty times and you didn't answer. What if I was abducted and locked in the trunk of someone's car?"
"Were you abducted, Holly?"
"No, but I can't find the Scotch tape and I need to attach a feather to the end of a pen. Did you put it somewhere?"

Immigration

When I moved to the United States, I had to complete several hundred forms, write several large cheques, and attend an interview during which Holly and I were tested, in separate rooms, to see if we were living as a married couple.

"What side of the bed does your wife sleep on?"
"From which direction? Looking out from in bed, Holly is on my left. But if you were standing at the foot of the bed looking at us, I'd be on your left."
"No, you do it like a car. From where you're sitting."
"Oh, that makes sense."
"So your answer is left?"
"Actually, it's more in the middle. I usually only have a few feet or so. Sometimes Holly sleeps diagonally though."
"I'll just mark it down as left. Next question. Describe your bed linen."
"Wrinkly."

I think you're meant to take sheets out of the dryer as soon as it stops spinning but who does that? It's like leaving the dishwasher and washing machine open when you're not using them so they don't get smelly. Who's walking around their house as if everything is perfectly normal with appliance doors open?

Cats

Our project manager, Rebecca, sews outfits for her cat Jack. I'm not sure why. I guess she was just sitting around one day and thought, "Fuck this shit, I'm forty and single, time Jack had a Peter Pan costume."

"And here's a close up showing the detail on his felt hat."
"Right, but what's it for?"
"What do you mean?"
"Is it for a costume party or something?"
"He's Peter Pan!"
"Yes, I can see that, but why?"
"Because it's adorable!"
"Okay."
"And here's one of him sleeping."

I've seen photos of Jack dressed as a pirate, a fireman, a cowboy, a fish, and a vampire. He's one of those fluffy cats with the pushed in face, the kind that stares at you with disgust as if to say, "Who invited you to Endor?"

I'm not a fan of any cats but if I'm watching a news report about one being rescued from a burning building and it turns out to be the fluffy pushed in face kind, I'm particularly disappointed.

Mugs

A few years back, our human resources manager, Jennifer, signed the office up for a five kilometre staff walk to promote Alzheimer's Awareness. Jennifer's father suffered from it so we all feigned caring. Apparently he'd once caught a taxi to the airport and waited fourteen hours for his wife, who had died several years earlier, to come out of the women's bathroom. Which is a bit sad but at least he's not putting cats in ovens and we've all had to wait outside of airport bathrooms.

I figured I'd stroll along with everyone for a bit, fall behind, and go home. I'm not capable of walking five kilometres. I could probably manage on a bike if it was all downhill but I wouldn't because there'd be no way of getting back and I don't ride bikes because I'm not ten. Melissa, our secretary, was assigned the task of organizing team t-shirts featuring the company name and logo for us to wear on the day. Apparently the website was confusing or something because she ordered coffee mugs instead.

I made a point of taking and walking with mine, holding it up as if to say 'cheers' each time Melissa looked my way, but that got old surprisingly quickly and the mug was annoying to carry so I left it in someone's letter box.

I'd like to think the person who checked their mail that day was delighted to find a free yellow mug with *Your Company Logo Here* emblazoned across it. It was a pretty big mug so perhaps they use it to eat soup out of.

"Margaret, have you seen my big yellow mug? The one I got in the mail?"
"It's in the dishwasher."
"Oh no, I was going to have some soup."
"We have soup bowls."
"Yes, but I didn't want a whole bowl of soup, just a big mug."
"What about the stoneware pottery mugs? They're pretty big."
"No, they're too gritty. I'll just go without."

Pet Names

My family wasn't very good at naming pets. We had a dog named Asparagus and, at one point, a cat named Heather Locklear Ballerina Disney. My sister was told she could name the cat but that doesn't mean agreeing to the first thing that pops out of her mouth. Whenever anybody asked me what the cat's name was, I told them it was Buck Rogers, which is a much better name.

Heather Locklear Ballerina Disney eventually hung herself on a Venetian blind cord and was replaced by Heather Locklear Ballerina Disney 2. After Heather Locklear Ballerina Disney 2 went missing, a rule was made about selecting pet names that aren't too embarrassing to put on lost posters but it wasn't adhered to, our next cat was named Susan.

Susan died when a sheet of metal roofing my father was replacing fell and sliced her in half. It didn't actually slice her completely in half; there was still about an inch of flesh holding Susan's two halves together, and she didn't die instantly. She managed to drag herself several feet in the time it took my father to climb down from the roof and finish her off with a shovel.

Backrubs

Backrubs are a form of currency in our house. They range from five minutes for emptying the kitchen bin to thirty minutes for doing the vacuuming.

Both Holly and I hate doing the vacuuming. We bought one of those little robot vacuum cleaners but what they don't show you in the commercial is all the banging into furniture and beeping when it gets stuck. I'd rather suck the dust up with a straw than listen to the horrible thing whirring around banging and beeping for two hours.

You also have to pick everything up off the floor before it runs, and clean it out every time it's finished. If we leave the house with it running, it manages to clean approximately four square inches before getting stuck. Once we found it upside down and another time it disappeared for a week when we left the back door open.

Rocket Bike

When I was in fourth grade, I told everyone at school my father was a motorcycle stuntman. I'm not sure why. I'd watched a television documentary about Evel Knievel around that time, so maybe that had something to do with it.

"Your dad works at the post office with my dad."
"Yes, Matthew, he hurt his leg in a crash so he's having a short break from stunt riding. When his leg is better, he's going to jump fifty buses to break the world record."
"You've never said anything about this before."
"That's because it's meant to be a secret. The bus companies don't like people jumping their buses. If you crash, it dents the roof."
"Your dad doesn't even have a motorcycle."
"Yes he does, Matthew, a Super Honda 5000 rocket bike. It's in the shed. That's why you haven't seen it."
"Can I come over and see it then?"
"When?"
"After school today?"
"No, I can't today. I have ninja practice."

To change the subject, I told Matthew that I was having a birthday party in a few weeks. It was nowhere near my birthday. Word quickly got around and, cornered by the lie, I confirmed to around twenty kids that yes, I was having a birthday party and yes, they could come. I was enjoying the attention at this stage. To add realism, I provided each a sheet from a pad of party invites with my address and a date set a few weeks away, figuring this would give me plenty of time to think of a reason to cancel. I forgot all about it until the first guests arrived. My father was watching cricket on television while my mother was out doing the weekly shopping.

I pretended there'd been a mix-up and I'd accidently written the incorrect day and month on twenty invites but I don't think anyone bought it. Also, one of the kids asked my father if he was really a motorcycle stunt man and if they could see his rocket bike in the shed.

Survival

I tried growing my own vegetables once. It was after watching a show called *Preppers* in which people wearing Wrangler jeans anticipate social collapse. I paid around $30 for seeds, $100 for railway ties, and $250 for fifty bags of garden soil which means the two cucumbers I ended up with cost $190 each. They weren't even good cucumbers. One was only an inch in length and the other had a huge grub living inside it. Should the grid ever 'go down', I estimate my chances of long-term survival as slim at best. I'll probably be shot at the supermarket and have my cans of evaporated milk and instant coffee taken from me on the first day.

My coworker Simon once told me that he really wished there would be a zombie apocalypse like in the show, The Walking Dead.
"I'd use a bow, or crossbow," he said, "Like Darryl. Because it's quieter."
"Sure," I agreed, "But the reload is dreadful. You'd probably be better off with a shotgun. Even if it is a bit louder. You don't have to be a very good aim with a shotgun."
Simon smiled and shook his head, "That's why I'd be a main character and you'd be one of the new people that joins our community then gets bitten and turns into a zombie that I have to shoot. With an arrow."

I recently asked my coworker Ben what he'd do if civilization collapsed, and he told me he'd go to a deserted island to wait it out. Which sounds nice but I'm not sure how he'd get there or how he'd survive. He has no boating experience and he doesn't eat meat or fish. Once, while eating lunch, Ben discovered a bit of bacon in his salad and gagged so badly he couldn't breathe and had to lie on the floor.

"What are you going to eat on your island, Ben? Bark?"
"No, I'll eat coconuts. They're high in protein and fibre."
"I'm sure they are. Plus you can make monkeys out of the shells when you get bored. For company."
"I won't be bored, I'll be too busy doing island things."
"Like what?"
"Swimming and relaxing."
"Well that sounds nice. Ignoring the fact you don't own a boat and have no navigation experience, I'm surprised you haven't left already."
"If the virus gets bad, I'll just steal a boat."
"You'll steal someone's boat?"
"Yes, from a jetty."
"And just point it out to sea, hit go, and hope you come across an island with coconuts?"
"I have Google Maps."

I asked the same question to a few other coworkers. Walter stated he'd go camping and live off squirrels and Gary said, "If it means never having to listen to conversations about coconut islands again, I hope I die."

Rebecca had the only viable plan; she'd head to her father's cabin. When Rebecca's mother passed away from cancer five years ago, her father sold the family home, purchased five acres of lakeside property, and had a wood cabin built. Apparently it has solar panels and a water purification system so, if you had enough supplies or liked to fish, you could theoretically hunker down there indefinitely. Rebecca's father spent his days fishing, cutting firewood, and writing a novel about a sentient crab, until he had a heart attack while trying to pull-start the motor on his dinghy.

It was a couple of weeks before Rebecca drove up to check on him so I assume it was a closed casket. Rebecca planned to keep and use the property for a year or two, then sell it. She invited everyone from work to spend the 4th of July there last year and, while I didn't go, I still have the address she emailed me. As such, Rebecca's plan to head to her father's cabin if the shit hits the fan is also my plan. I'll get there first and change the locks.

"Let me in, I have nowhere else to go."
"Perhaps you should have thought about that before you told Mike I forged his signature to order an office parrot."

When I was in grade eight or nine, our class watched a movie called *The Day After*, about a nuclear attack and the aftermath that follows. There's a scene where a family is in a bunker or basement rationing food, and, after watching the movie, our teacher had us write an assignment about who we'd let in to our bunker if space and food was limited, and why. Most of the class wrote that they would include their parents, siblings, friends and pets - maybe their grandparents and relatives. I chose Jeannie from *I Dream of Jeannie* and I still stand by my choice.

These days, if I had to choose who to let into a bunker, I'd probably only include my partner Holly and my offspring Seb. Even those two are iffy. Seb eats and shits his own weight every few hours, and Holly would want to bring the dogs, Trivial Pursuit, and her karaoke machine into the bunker. I'd rather stay outside and take my chances to be honest.

"Who's up for karaoke?"
"Actually, I was just about to head out. Might scavenge for food amongst the ruins while fending off giant mutant radioactive cockroaches for a bit."
"How long will you be?"
"That depends on whether I'm captured by post-apocalyptic warlords or not."
"Okay. Bring back some toilet paper. We're almost out."

Toasted Sandwiches

A co-worker recently spent twenty minutes describing to me new curtains she had ordered for her living room due to the previous ones not working overly well with a rug. To understand the dilemma properly, the rug was also described in detail, along with the sofa fabric that the rug was purchased to match. I honestly wouldn't care if she lived at the bottom of the ocean with giant squid for curtains.

I nodded in an attentive manner but was actually thinking about oxy-acetylene welders and all the things I could make if I owned one. Afterwards, I looked up welders on Amazon but they were far too expensive so I bought a Breville sandwich maker instead.

"Dad, what's for dinner?"
"Toasted sandwiches."
"Again? We had toasted sandwiches yesterday. And the day before that. We've had them every day for the past week."
"They've had different fillings. That's the beauty of toasted sandwiches, the contents are limited only by imagination."
"They've all been cheese."
"Yes, but they've been different brands of cheese. It's not my problem if your palate isn't refined enough to tell the difference between Kraft and Cracker Barrel."

Seattle Real Estate

"So it's a cardboard box on the side of a street?"
"Yes, but check out the view. Location, location, location."
"And they're asking how much?"
"It's listed at six-hundred-thousand but there may be some wriggle room as the seller is motivated."
"What about HOA fees?"
"Four-hundred per week but that includes use of the pool."
"There's a pool?"
"Technically it's a puddle but it's yours to use whenever you like. When it rains. Which is quite often. That's why the box has a tarp over it."

Beaches

Brochures always show beaches deserted, possibly with a footprint in the sand, but they're never like that. I'd probably quite like the beach if there weren't any people. Or sharks. A private beach would be quite nice, a few steps from a mansion of something. I still wouldn't go in the water but I might sit in a deck chair eating a sandwich while looking out at the water. Probably wondering how many sharks are in it. Then I'd head back up to my mansion and check my stocks while wearing a white bathrobe.

Once, while at the beach wading with my offspring, I was hit in the head by a surfboard. The next few moments were a semi-conscious blur of waves crashing and losing my shorts while being pulled out of the water by a lifeguard and I recovered lying on the beach in the centre of an applauding crowd with my genitals covered by an old lady's sun hat. Wrapping a borrowed Spongebob Squarepants towel around my lower half, I waded back into the water in search of my shorts and was stung by a jellyfish.

I went to the beach again recently, after managing to avoid the horrid process for several years, and regardless of the fact that there is no logical purpose for a bee to be at the beach, I was stung by one on the face.

Rabies

I was a skinny child and quite self-conscious of my scrawny frame. I avoided any environment where I would have to take my shirt off in public, such as the beach or swimming pools, and I forged dozens of notes to get out of showering at gym in high school.

"David, this note states you have smallpox."
"Yes. Just on my chest though, that's why I can't take my shirt off."
"Smallpox was eradicated in the early nineteen hundreds."
"It's a different type of smallpox. Smallerpox."
"Right. Last week you had rabies."
"Yes, a bat bit my chest."

Tiny Houses

I saw a show on television tonight called *Tiny House Hunters*. It was about poor people who have decided to decrease the square footage of their living area from two or three thousand square feet to under two hundred by moving to live in a camper trailer. None of them said, "I'm poor and I'm going to live a trailer" of course, they justified their decision by claiming environmental responsibility, or the desire not to be part of the mortgage rat-race, or a love of being able to hitch up their house and travel wherever they want. None of them travelled anywhere though, they parked their 'tiny house' on their parent's property. Which their parents must be fucking delighted about.

"You've bought a house? I'm proud of you. I was wondering when you were going to make your way out into the world on your own. You're forty-five after all."
"Yes, as of this morning, I'm officially a home owner. It's a lot of responsibility but I'm ready to take it on."
"Well, if you need any help moving your stuff let me know."
"That won't be necessary, there isn't room for any of my stuff in the new house so I'm going to leave it all here."
"What if you need something?"
"I'll walk across and get it. I'm parking my house in the backyard. Do we have any spare extension cables?"

Charades

I wasn't a fan of staying at my auntie's house when I was a young; she made my sister and I do chores. Not small chores like changing the kitty litter or taking the trash out either; she had us tile her bathroom and sand & stain floorboards. Once, she made me re-concrete loose chimney bricks on her roof. Worse than that, was the fact that she didn't own a television. Instead, we played charades.

"First word... The."
"Second word... fingers? No? ... counting? No? Oh, six?"
"mmhmm"
"Okay, third word... sounds like... dancing? No? Electric shock? No? Wriggling? No? I give up."
"I was jiggling!"
"Why didn't you just nod and tap your nose when I said wriggling then? Wriggling rhymes with jiggling."
"Oh yeah."
"The six jiggling what?"
"No, jiggling 'sounds like' million."
"*The Six Million Dollar Man*?"
"Yes!"
"Jiggling doesn't sound anything like million."
"It does if you say it like 'jigilin.'"

Facebook

My partner Holly has over a thousand 'friends' on Facebook. Sometimes when she posts a photo, someone will comment and I'll ask who that person is and Holly will reply with, "I don't know. I think he was the assistant rep for a company that did subcontract work for a company that used to do the printing for the company that the people who did our flyers used." So it's probably really someone Holly dated before she met me. Why would anyone write, "Looks great!" in response to a post about our new deck unless there was some kind of history there? Keep it in your pants, Todd McNamara.

I'm not a fan of Facebook as it mostly consists of people posting stuff they did when I wasn't there. If I wasn't there, I don't care. If it seems like something I might have enjoyed being there for, fuck you for not inviting me. A photo of your cat? Didn't need to be there. The cat looks like every other cat on the planet. A photo of you drinking beer around a fire pit with a dozen other people I know? I hope someone throws a bag of gunpowder and nails in.

I usually unfriend people the second they post religious quotes, photos of cats, stuff about mistreated dogs, photos of their car, photos of their haircut, photos of them playing frisbee golf, and anything to do with movember, astrology, or fun runs. There's no real rule, it depends on my mood on the day. I unfriended someone this morning because my arm hurt. Yesterday, I unfriended someone because she asked for Netflix recommendations. If I have to scroll endlessly through the Netflix's stupid interface before making a selection, so can everyone else. I'm not Roger Ebert.

Having extended the 'unfriend' rule recently to anyone posting 'Stop the Steal' or anti-mask political statements, I now have a negative number of friends on Facebook - when I view the list, weird code runs down my screen for a few seconds and then my laptop explodes.

For a while I was just clicking the 'unfollow' button, but people you unfollow don't know you've unfollowed them which doesn't send much of a message.

"Did you unfriend me on Facebook?"
"Yes."
"Why?"
"Because I don't like you anymore. I'm not sure that I ever did really. I only accepted your friend request so I could see your photos and they're boring."
"Wow. Thanks, Dad. Having a bad day?"
"Yes, my arm hurts."

Spring Onions

I went eight weeks without leaving the house recently. When I eventually had to, to purchase non-droopy spring onions, it took me an hour to get dressed, as I had no idea what I used to wear in public, and I had to relearn how to operate a motor vehicle. I blame the gear shifter in my car for the dent in our garage. Instead of a normal shifter in the console, I have a round knob on the dashboard, right next to the stereo. It's only a matter of time before I'm doing eighty, attempt to change the music volume, and put the vehicle into reverse.

Thankfully, access to delivery services such as Instacart means I rarely need to leave the house to buy groceries. For those unfamiliar with Instacart, a 'personal shopper' drives to the supermarket, does all your shopping for you, and delivers the groceries to your front door. You then give them an eighty-cent tip and a bad rating through the Instacart app because they selected droopy spring onions.

"What's for dinner?"
"Nothing. The spring onions are droopy."
"Not every meal needs a chopped spring onion sprinkle."
"Of course it does. It's about presentation. Without a spring onion sprinkle, I may as well serve dinner in a bucket. Or just throw it on the floor. Is that how we live now?"

Tractors

I'm not a fan of country music. The one that goes "You don't have to be lonely, at Farmersonly.com" is okay though. It's pretty catchy and the video clip has fat girls wearing rubber boots and milking cows - two of my three fetishes. I do understand we can't all have the same tastes in music though; I grew up in the eighties listening to New Order and Human League, while my friend JM grew up listening to his grandmother screaming, "Your pigs are loose again, JM!"

"Right, if you are going to bitch about the song so much, I'll change it."
"No, leave it, JM. If you change it now I'll never find out if the rain eventually came and saved his crops."
"It's not about the crops, it's about his love of the land. Here, listen to this one..."
"...It's the same song. I recognize the bottle-cap stick."
"It's a different song. Listen to the words goddammit."
"Is this one also about farming?"
"Shut the fuck up and listen to it. How can you criticize a song if you don't listen to the lyrics?"
"That's where our music requirements differ, I like a bit of bass with a drop and a tune. I don't give a fuck how much a farmer loves his land. I'd assume he'd get another job if he didn't."

JM's favorite farm-emo singer is a hairy guy named David Allan Coe who looks like he probably lives in a log cabin in the woods that his granpappy built and owns a lot of guns. His most famous song is about driving his pickup truck to collect his mother from prison but, before he gets there, she's run over by a train. It's pretty much up there with the classics like *Achy Breaky Heart* by Hannah Montana's dad and Kenny Chesney's *She Thinks My Tractor's Sexy*.

For those not familiar with *She Thinks My Tractor's Sexy*, here are the lyrics:

Plowing these fields in the hot summer sun.
Over by the gate yonder here she comes.
With a basket full of chicken and a big cold jug of sweet tea.
I make a little room and she climbs on up,
I open up the throttle and stir a little dust.
Look at her face, she ain't a foolin' me,
she thinks my tractor's sexy.
It really turns her on.

It's basically the musical equivalent of *Fifty Shades of Grey* for farmers. Yes, Cletus, everyone thinks your tractor is hot. And your oversized Carhartt jacket and Wrangler boot-cut jeans with pig shit stains on the cuffs. When you're blocking traffic doing 15mph on a single lane road, we're definitely all thinking, "I'd love to give that tractor driver some chicken," and not, "Pull over and let us pass, you leather-faced old fuck, we've got places to be."

I actually drove a tractor once. Technically I just steered it while sitting on a farmer's lap but it still counts. It was on one of those 'pick your own strawberries' farms. I wrote about the experience for a 'what I did on school break' assignment a few weeks later, but left out the part about the farmer being on the tractor with me and added something about rescuing a lost lamb.

My English teacher, Mrs Bowman, could have just left it, but decided to call me out about why the farmer would let me drive off on a tractor by myself, and how I knew how to throw a lasso to drag the lamb out of quicksand. I told her the farmer was busy planting corn and I learned lasso twirling from my uncle, who was a cowboy, but she called bullshit and brought in a rope the next day for me to demonstrate to the class.

Surprisingly, I was naturally gifted at rope handling and managed to lasso a chair from across the room. My classmates cheered and the teacher apologised for doubting my story and gave me an A for my assignment. Later that day, I saved a school bus full of children from going over a cliff by lassoing the bumper just in time.

No, not really, when presented with the rope, I mumbled something about it not being the right kind for lassoing, and Mrs Bowman instructed me to sit down and told a story to the class about a boy who lies and doesn't find money behind dusty jam jars so can't buy a bike.

I can't recall the exact details of the story but basically a boy, apparently named David, is saving up to buy a bike. He asks a farmer if he has any chores he needs doing and the farmer tells David that if he changes the straw in the chicken coop and cleans the dust off a high shelf of jam jars, he will pay David two dollars. David agrees to what is essentially child labor and heads off to the chicken coop. There was a lot of straw so David, figuring the farmer wouldn't be able to tell the difference, just throws some new straw on top of the old straw to save himself some work. He then heads to the special shelf where the farmer keeps his jam jars, and dusts only the ones in front that are visible. Thinking he's oh so clever, David heads back to the farmer, states that he has finished the chores, and asks to be paid. The farmer puts on an act about being puzzled, because he left the money on the job sites, and makes David follow him back to the chicken coop where he lifts up the straw, new and old, and shows David a dollar on the dirt. The farmer then checks the jam jars and shows David a dollar inside a dusty jar at the back.

At this point, anyone else would have said, "Weird that you were able to set all that up before I even asked you about doing chores, but okay, you got me, keep your two dollars you trap-setting old cunt," but apparently David just hung his head in shame and walked home. Also, the next day, David asked several different farmers if they had any chores for him to do, but word had gotten around about his half-arsedness and David never got his bike. Or he learned his lesson and eventually got his bike. I can't remember how the story ended, or what the point of it was, probably not to trust farmers.

It's true, you can't trust farmers. Once, when our class went on an excursion to a dairy farm, a farmer told me cows communicate to each other telepathically and I believed it for several years. I mean, why would a farmer make that up? Sorry your job is so boring you have to lie to eight-year-olds but perhaps you should consider the repercussions of when they're fourteen and arguing with a biology teacher because they were given false information by a professional in the milk industry.

Windows

Our neighbours across the street have a cat that stares out of their front window all day. I've never seen the cat outside so I assume it's an interior only one. Like certain paints or cushions that haven't been Scotchgarded.

Last week, while I was standing at our front window looking out, I realized the cat and I were doing the same thing. We were like mirror images or goldfish in distant bowls. We stared across the street at each other for a few minutes, then I waved, and I swear the cat waved back.

It's possible he was just swiping at a moth or something, or perhaps I experienced a mild form of cabin fever and imagined it. I did have a dream that night about the cat giving me a haircut. It was the best haircut I'd ever had and I remember thinking in my dream, 'I should take a photo of this haircut so I can recreate it,' but then deciding that wasn't neccessary because I'd just get the cat to cut it every time.

It's also possible the cat, caught off guard, waved and then thought, 'Fuck, I'm not meant to interact like that. Stay cool and he'll think I was swiping at a moth or something.'

Goth

Most of us grew out of the Goth thing in the eighties. Fat girl Goths held out the longest as it meant relinquishing their point of difference and going back to being normal fat girls again.

"Still a Goth I see, Susan."
"Please call me Duskblade. And yes."
"Well I admire your commitment. Not a lot of people are still sporting white face paint and black lipstick. You're the only Goth I've seen at the mall today. The only one I've seen since 1993 actually. Heading to Hot Topic to do a bit of shopping?"
"No, to the food court."

Schewel's

Ian stared out the window and sighed. Schewel's had given him a delivery estimate but it was very broad. 'Sometime between noon and five' meant he'd had to take the whole afternoon off work and he was very busy; there were boxes to be lifted and put back down in a different spot. It wasn't work that anyone could do either. Someone with only one arm couldn't do it for example. A young child wouldn't even be able to get their arms around the boxes. Someone that didn't know what a box was, or how to pick things up and put them down in a different spot, would also have difficulty.

He played his banjo while he waited. Then pickled some beans. He was watching *Delta Force 2* from his Chuck Norris collection on VHS when the delivery people finally arrived. "Anywhere is fine," he told them, "As long as it's facing the television."

The sectional had cost two hundred dollars, almost a week's pay, but it was worth every cent. It was a lot nicer than David's living room furniture. David's furniture was rectangular and uncomfortable looking and didn't have cup holders in the armrests.

Staff Retreat

I attended a staff retreat once. While I was there, Lillian, our senior designer, set fire to a hut and destroyed two kayaks with an axe.

She was in love with Thomas, the owner of the agency, and while Thomas was passed out drunk the first night, Lillian went through his phone messages and learned he'd had sex with the Asian lady who cleans his apartment.

It was a one-time thing, and had cost Thomas two hundred dollars, but it had happened on the same day that Lillian made him cabbage soup for lunch at work.

Falling Water

"Thanks for meeting us on site, Frank."
"No problem."
"What we're looking for is a small holiday cabin about fifty-feet from the river."
"Gotcha, *on* the river."
"No, fifty-feet from the edge. So we can see the river and waterfall while we're relaxing on the patio."
"You'd still be able to see the river if I built the house on it, you'd just have to stand up and look down over the balcony."
"That doesn't sound very practical. I'd like to be able to see the river while I'm sitting down."
"I could add a glass floor bit for you to look through."
"That's hardly the same as being able to see the whole river, is it? We'd just see water running underneath. What about the waterfall?"
"It's not that great. I've seen bigger ones. Besides, if you're over the waterfall, you'll be able to hear it better."
"I'm just not sure it's…"
"Right, you know what? I don't think I want to build it at all anymore."
"Don't be like that, Frank. Fine, we'll discuss the location of the house later and maybe come up with some kind of compromise."

"No, I'm going home. There's heaps of other projects I'd much rather be working on."

"Okay, you can build it on the river."

"Really?"

"Yes. Now, for the materials, we were thinking either cedar or redwood."

"Gotcha, twelve-thousand tons of cantilevered reinforced concrete."

"Sorry?"

"Nothing."

"We want it in either cedar or redwood, Frank."

"Sure. So what's your budget for this project?"

"Thirty-five thousand."

"Okay, so somewhere between thirty-five thousand and two-hundred thousand. I can work with that. Oh, by the way, how do you feel about really low ceilings?"

"We'd like really grand ceilings, at least twelve-feet."

"Got it."

Pool Float

I once gave my sister Leith five hundred dollars, to fix the transmission on her van, and she bought an above ground pool instead. I never saw a cent of the money again and I never went for a swim because, well, it was an above ground pool.

Even if you build a deck around an above ground pool, everyone knows what it is. Nobody says, "Oh really? It's an above ground pool? You'd never be able to tell." They say, "Oh, the invite didn't mention it's an above ground pool. I wouldn't have come if I'd known."

Maybe not to your face but that's what they're saying.

Leith didn't have a deck around her pool so everyone just sat in Coleman camping chairs looking up at it. I mentioned the money a few years later and Leith stated, "I bought you a pool float."

Badminton

I died when I was ten. My father didn't know CPR but he tried blowing into my mouth and hitting my chest while my mother, grandparents, sister and cousins stood in a ring around me waiting for the ambulance to arrive.

I had a dream while I was dead. I was swimming and the water turned to solid ice. There weren't any lights or tunnels like I have heard other people describe, just ice. I could see my arms below the surface but I couldn't move them. My legs were also trapped but the frozen layer stopped at my ankles, leaving my feet free to move in the water below. I saw a large dark shape swimming under me. It brushed my left foot.
"David!"
There was suddenly a lot of noise. Sirens, yelling, beeping.
"He's conscious."

Badminton is a stupid game and people look stupid while they're playing it. My cousin Susan, a large girl, played competitive badminton for a team. Who plays badminton for a team? It's a game for backyards and bored children. She and I were playing against each other at her house during a family gathering the day I died. The adults were inside eating fondue and listening to Boney-M records.

I'd never played badminton before and the fact that Susan was losing by several points was making her quite upset. She blamed the wind direction, and her shoes, and how spongy the grass was. I suggested it might be because the game is easy and stupid and not a real sport like tennis.

"Of course it's a real sport. What would you know?"
"I know I'm winning even though I've never played before."
"Only because this isn't my regular racquet."
"This isn't my regular racquet either."
"I'm actually just letting you win. I usually play really well. I've got a trophy."
"Really? For badminton or pie eating?"

My sister and I were under strict instructions never to mention Susan's weight. We'd been told that she had a medical condition or something but every time I saw her, she had a mouth full of chips, cake or sausage. It wasn't just 'big bones', she had no neck. She looked like a slug, with other slugs for legs and arms.

Susan lost it. She kicked over one of the poles that was holding up the badminton net and threw her racquet into the air. It landed on the roof of the house. She glared at me, gave me the finger, and stormed inside. My sister had been waiting to play the winner and groaned about the loss of the racquet.

"You'll have to go up there and get it," she said.

"I'm not going up there," I replied. It was a two-story house.
"Oh, go on. If you climb on to the water tank, you should be able to reach that tree branch which goes up to the roof. It looks easy."
"You do it then."
"I'm wearing sandals."
"Fine."

Making it up *was* actually easy. I stepped from the branch onto the roof and edged my way along the slope to the racquet.

I heard the front door slam. "Where's David?" yelled my father. My sister pointed. He craned his head around and up.

"What the fuck are you doing up there?"
I held the racquet up to show him.
"Did you call Susan fat?"
"No, she said she had a trophy and I asked if it was for eating pies."
"Right, you're in big fucking trouble. Get down here now. You're going to go in there and apologise to her in front of everybody."
"No."
I'd have spent the rest of my life on the roof rather than face the humiliation of apologising in front of everybody.
"Don't make me come up there."

I sat down.

It had taken me about five minutes to get up, it took my father less than one. He was also wearing sandals so I call bullshit on my sister's excuse. I panicked, looking for another way down as he stepped off the branch. There was a concrete driveway below me but on the other side of that was a garage. I decided, given enough run-up, I would be able to make it. From there, it would be a simple task to drop onto the neighbouring property fence and escape through their yard. My father edged along the sloping roof towards me. I backed up a bit, ran, and jumped.

I mostly blame the incline as you need a flat area for a decent run up. Also, as I stepped on the edge of the roof and leapt, the gutter gave way, cancelling any propulsion upwards. I flailed. I have a vague recollection of what concrete looks like as it rushes towards you at high speed but I don't remember the impact.

I was in surgery for eight hours and in hospital for three months. The right side of my skull had been fractured, shattered really, several fragments were removed from my brain. My collar bone, right arm, six ribs and left foot were also broken but brain trauma was the main concern.

I forgot things. Not all things, just some things. Things like bath plugs and rabbits. I had all of my motor skills and could remember the name of every *Star Wars* character, but I had no idea what a blender was or what a round, orange coloured fruit was called. I knew the colour orange but there was a broken link somewhere. It didn't concern me that much, I understood that I had forgotten things but I had no idea what things they were until I came across them and then it was just as if I had never known about that particular thing in the first place.

"What's this thing? Is it a belt?"
"No, it's called a leash. It connects to a dog's collar so you can take the dog for a walk without it running away."
"Clever."

A man with a grey beard and blue glasses visited me regularly in the hospital to play games. His name was Henry. The games mainly consisted of naming the item pictured on cards he held up. He'd pause often and scribble in a notebook. Sometimes he would sing parts of songs and ask me to finish them.

"Bathroom tiles?"
"Okay. What else is white?"
"The lamb?"
"Well yes, but you wouldn't say Mary's lamb is as white as the lamb. What else could a lamb be as white as? Something white and cold..."
"A glass of milk?"

For the first few weeks, I shared a room with another boy my age named Mark. He only had one arm. Apparently he had opened a top loading washing machine lid while it was in spin cycle and reached in to grab an item of clothing. His arm was twisted off at the shoulder. Sometimes when Henry would ask me a question or hold up a picture, Mark would answer for me and say things like, "Oh my god, I can't believe you don't know what a turtle is. Everybody knows what a turtle is," so Henry moved me to a different room by myself.

It was a smaller room, white with no window or television. There was a painting on the wall of a beach at sunset but Henry took it down. I read a lot of books. There wasn't anything else to do. Henry gave me a highlighter pen and asked me to mark any words I came across that I didn't know but it was easy to cheat by looking up the words in a dictionary. Sometimes when Henry visited, he was accompanied by three or four other people. While Henry and I played games, they stood in a corner watching. Occasionally he would ask them a question and there would be a discussion about things such as ventral streams and parietal lobes. The term Agnosia was used a lot.

"Snow."
"Very good. And can you describe snow for me?"
"Frozen water crystals that fall if the temperature is low enough. It's fluffy and white. Like lamb fleece."
"And can you tell me what this is a picture of?"
"A turtle."

My parents took me home. Every few weeks I met with Henry for an hour or so but these meetings eventually became shorter and less frequent. I returned to school. Over the next few years, the instances when I would hear a word or discover an item that was new to me became less constant but again, I wasn't to know if I had always not known them.

It came in handy sometimes. I would pretend not to know what a vacuum cleaner or lawn mower was. Before the accident, I used to get dropped off at my piano teacher's house ever Thursday night for an hour. Her name was Mrs Williams. For the first half-hour she would yell at me for not practicing then spend the rest of the time talking about her fourteen cats. I had no idea what I was even meant to be learning. She said I was the worst student she had ever had. Sometimes she would call me Dennis and make me fix stuff around the house. Once, she made me run a bath and help her in. I would have told my parents but they might have made me go to a different teacher and then I would have had to learn to play the piano. After the accident, I just pretended to not know what a piano was.

I hadn't lost ten years of things. Just things dotted amongst that ten years. It didn't take ten years to reknow these things either, if I had ever known them. From age ten and up it is easier to grasp things than it is at four or five. I eventually stopped playing 'did I know this?' with myself. Like everyone else, there were just things I know, things I have never known, and things I have forgotten. I may have once known what a Lychee is but it doesn't matter, I'm not going to buy one anyway.

Cheese

I'm not a fan of Brie. It's pale with a grayish tinge under a rind of white mould. I'll take a Kraft single over mouldy or sloppy soft cheeses any day. I don't care if that makes me a cheese philistine. Enjoy your mouldy grey cheeses and sloppy soft ones that look like baby vomit, I'll have a bit of Colby Jack if I'm feeling adventurous.

I read somewhere that blue vein cheese only became a thing during the Dark Ages when the inhabitants of a besieged castle ran out of food, were forced to eat mouldy cheese, and declared, "Not bad. I definitely prefer this over rat heads."

"Barry, try this cheese, it's delicious."
"No thanks, it's mouldy. I realise we're besieged and have run out of food but that doesn't mean we have to resort to eating rancid scraps. Is there anything else?"
"Just this pitcher of milk. It's curdled and gone blobby and smells a bit, but it tastes pretty good. Kind of like a sloppy soft cheese. Try it."
"No, I'm good."
"Suit yourself. By the way, how are the wife and kids?"
"They're fine. They have the plague but the King says it's just like a bad case of the flu and will go away in the warmer months like a miracle."

Pumpkins

Holly purchased four-hundred pumpkins for the front porch recently. So that people driving past can say, "Fuck that's a lot of pumpkins."

"How much did you actually spend on pumpkins, Holly?"
"Not much."
"What are they, like a dollar each?"
"Something like that."
"So about four-hundred dollars then?"
"There's not that many."
"Where did you even find this many pumpkins?"
"I went to a farm."
"What?"
"A pumpkin farm."
"Were they selling them from a cart out the front?"
"No, I picked them."
"Did the farmer see you?"
"Yes, you pay him to pick them. He gives you a cart and a pair of stalk cutters and you walk around and pick the ones you like. It's not a thing in Australia?"
"No. People generally just buy one pumpkin at a time. From a supermarket. If they're making a soup or something."
"You don't decorate your porch in fall?"
"No."

"Well that's just sad."
"Not particularly. You don't think it's weird stacking four-hundred pumpkins on a porch?"
"It's festive."
"It's a bit over the top."
"No it isn't. I actually need a few more to fill in the gaps."
"How did you even get this many pumpkins home?"
"I rented a truck from Lowe's."

Someone stopped last week because they thought we were selling them. I gave them a pumpkin for their trouble, figuring we had plenty, but Holly noticed there was one missing when she got home. Apparently it was the best pumpkin in the world and her entire display was ruined. As she was pretty cross about it, I denied any knowledge as to the pumpkin's whereabouts and suggested that perhaps someone had stolen it to make a soup. We have one of those Ring Video Doorbell systems installed now. It cost two-hundred-dollars but can you really put a price on being protected from pumpkin bandits?

I work from home a lot and Holly has access to the Ring on her phone while she's at work so, for the first week after it was installed, I received texts from her every few minutes to let me know that, "The mail just came" and, "There's a cat outside."

I've been accused of exaggerating before so here's a complete list of Holly's security updates during the first day:

9.17am "Can you clean the Ring lens please? It's blurry."
9.22am "That's better. Thank you."
9.24am "Stand in the driveway and wave."
9.26am "Did you cut your hair?"
10.16am "Squirrel on the porch!"
10.18am "Never mind, it's gone now."
10.21am "We should trim the bushes in the front yard."
10.26am "UPS delivered a box. What did you order?"
10.42am "We should get a bird-feeder."
10.44am "The mail came."
11.06am "Has the Ring frozen?"
11.08am "Never mind. I just saw a car drive past."
11.28am "There's a cat outside."
11.34am "It's still there."
11.39am "I watched you put a piece of tape over the lens."
11.43am "Can you take it off please?"
1.22pm "I'm serious."
1.43pm "I'm getting really angry."
2.02pm "Thank you."
2.07pm "Can you move that please? Where did you even get a cardboard cutout of Jonah Hill?"

Art Students

I knew an art student named Becca once, she was dating my housemate and you could tell when she stayed over by the smell of patchouli. All art students wear patchouli as it's a magic repellant against criticism and having to get a real job. We had one of Becca's paintings on the wall of our living room. It was titled *Self Portrait 28*.

"It's pretty big," I commented when it was first hung.
"A large statement deserves a large canvas," Becca explained.
"So, it's you on a horse?"
"It's an expression of joy, movement, and freedom."
"Shouldn't the horse be in motion then? It's just standing there looking anything but joyful. Is it crying?"
"They're tears of happiness. And the horse *is* in motion."
"Its legs would be bent if it was in motion."
"It's jumping."
"Straight up?"
"It's easy to criticise."
"Correct."
"An inability to interpret art says a lot more about the viewer than the artist. It's not my job to explain."
"Granted. You weren't overly helpful with the title though, you should have called it *Rebecca's Happy Hover Horse*."

Eskimo Day

Seb paused his game of *War of the Monsters* and yelled into the kitchen, "Oh yeah, I almost forgot, tomorrow's Eskimo day at school."
He was five and it was way past his bedtime.
"What the fuck is Eskimo Day?" I yelled back.
"Everyone has to dress like an Eskimo."
"Oh my god, Seb. It's almost ten o'clock."

We pulled it off but it was past three in the morning before we climbed into our beds. A large faux-fur blanket had been sacrificed to create the overshirt; I cut out two T shapes and hand-sewed them together. A half circle of the same blanket stitched to the neck line formed a fur hood. I made the fur boots the same way, hand stitching curved tubes that he could pull over his sneakers. For his spear, I removed the shower curtain rod and attached a butter knife to it with duct tape. It had all come together and wasn't half bad.

We were tired but made it to his school the next morning no later than our usual lateness, I walked him into his class wearing his outfit. It was 'Excursion Day' and everyone was dressed to go to a local quarry to learn about fossils. There was a permission slip in the bottom of his schoolbag that stated, 'please dress appropriately'.

Nacho Soup

My partner Holly can't cook. She's capable of the process of cooking, but she can't cook in the same way an octopus can't ride a bicycle; it has enough arms to reach the pedals and handlebars, but the result will rarely be a successful journey from A to B.

I once looked over Holly's shoulder to discover her crumbling Alka-Seltzer tablets into a meal she was preparing because "they are salty and we ran out of salt."

On Saturday evening, Holly stated that she was making nachos for dinner so I was surprised to be presented with a bowl and spoon an hour later.

"What's this?"
"The nachos were a bit runny so I added a few cups of water. It's nacho soup."
"Is there even such a thing? And what are these bits in it?"
"They're the chips," Holly stated defensively as she sipped a spoon of Nachos and made a long 'mmmmmm' noise, "I put it all in the blender so there shouldn't be any big bits."
"I'm ringing for pizza."
"Typical, you never appreciate anything I do."
"That's not true. I appreciate everything you do but if I

ordered a hamburger at McDonald's and they handed it to me in a cup with a straw saying 'Sorry, it was a bit runny so we threw it in the blender and added two cups of water, it's Big Mac soup', I would assume the restaurant was entirely staffed through some kind of special needs employment initiative. If they asked me, "Do you want fries with that?" I sure as fuck wouldn't reply, 'Yes, mix them in.'"

"It would probably be quite good," replied Holly, "but you would never know because you are too much of an asshole to taste it. Even if the guy at McDonalds spent an hour in the kitchen making it for you and burnt his thumb on a saucepan."

"Fine," I relented, taking a scoop and raising it to my mouth, "I'll taste it."

Sipping at the brown and yellow puree, I felt an intense burning sensation not unlike having a mouth full of red ants. I swallowed with effort as my eyes began to water.

"It's a bit spicy."

"Yes," replied Holly, "We were out of Cumin so I used Curry instead. It's like an Indian version of Nacho soup."

Japanese Porn

I discovered a porn folder on a coworker's computer recently. It was mostly Japanese Animé porn though, which was a bit disappointing.

One of the videos was about a woman with both male and female genitalia. She had a giant crystal sword and wore a bikini space suit for some reason. There was a lot of yelling and running fast, and a flashback to when she was a famous pop-singer, then she had sex with some kind of half man, half rock-monster, who also had both genitalia, while floating in space. When they reached climax, there was a lot of flashes and a planet exploded. Back on earth, a lady holding a small boy's hand pointed up at a bright light in the night sky, presumably the exploded planet even though there's no way light travels that fast, and the boy did a little excited running on the spot dance and shouted, "Naya nomble can!"

It was pretty dreadful but who am I to judge? I've closed browser windows and sat silently for a few moments thinking, 'What's wrong with me?' many times. The last time was after watching a Youtube video on how to build your own swimming pool out of railway ties.

Yemen

I've only ever met one person from Yemen, he owned a local falafel shop until he was arrested for riding a scooter drunk and deported for being in the country illegally. He's probably standing in rubble wearing a suit jacket right now, waving a AK47 in the air and yelling, "Wololololol" for no apparent reason.

I realize that's a bit stereotypical but if your country condones burying women up to their necks and throwing rocks at their heads for reading, you deserve to cop a bit of flak. I'm sorry your government and infrastructure is a mess, and that you're at war because your invisible sky wizard says it's okay to eat toast and someone else's invisible sky wizard says it's not, but yelling, "Wololololol" isn't going to fix anything. Sort it out.

Sure, 'sort it out' isn't exactly groundbreaking foreign policy, but honestly, if you've got time to stand around in rubble yelling, "Wololololol", you've got time to sweep up a bit. The ones that ride around in the back of a pickup truck yelling, "Wololololol" with fifteen other idiots aren't much better, but at least they're going somewhere. Hopefully to Home Depot to buy a few brooms and construction strength garbage bags.

Trapdoor

My father watched a lot of football and cricket on television when I was young. It's always either football or cricket season in Australia. I followed neither. He was watching the cricket the day my mother took my sister and I to the pool, the day he left. When my offspring Seb was six or seven, my father emailed me and wrote, "I know I wasn't a very good father but I'd like to try to be a good grandfather."

I suppose it was a turning point in his life. The woman he had left my mother for had left him to move in with a security guard named Gary after nearly two decades of marriage. They owned a house together, a large ranch-style home with a tennis court and swimming pool, no kids of their own. There was a large sign on the entry gate that read For Sale, Price Reduced.

I stopped the car for a moment, considered reversing back and driving home. I don't know why I'd said, "Okay, that sounds good," when he'd invited us to visit, because it hadn't. It sounded uncomfortable and weird. Not because I had any animosity, but because I simply didn't know him. I glanced over at Seb in the passenger seat, he was playing a game on his phone. I sighed and drove up the long gravel driveway, parking alongside a half-loaded Budget rental truck.

It was uncomfortable and weird. Seb had no idea who the old man asking for a hug was. I had no idea who the old man I was shaking hands with was. He was thinner than I remembered, pinker and greyer. The last time I had seen him I was eleven and he must have been in his thirties. He had a moustache back then, a large one the same as his favourite cricketer.

"Did you find the place okay?"
"Yes, we came up the main highway, turned at the Mobil."
"Ah. It's about five minutes quicker if you turn at the Shell before that."
"Really?"
"Yes. Less traffic."
"I'd remember that for next time but as you're moving, there's not much point."
"No, I suppose not."

He had a present for Seb which was a nice gesture.
The yellow, red and blue plastic cricket set was a little young for him but it's the thought that counts. Seb was old enough to know to act pleased.

Seb ran about the house exploring while I helped my father load boxes and furniture. There wasn't a lot of it. We didn't talk about anything that had happened over the last twenty-odd years. Which is a good thing I suppose. It was like two strangers chatting in a pub; polite 'sitting at the bar' conversation. There were awkward silences but carrying out boxes gave us an alternative to staring and nodding. He talked about football and cricket but I've never followed either. We talked about cars and the weather instead, and where he was moving to. It was meant to be a short visit. A test visit to see if there would be further visits. I don't know why I offered to help him move into his new house.

The new house didn't have a tennis court or swimming pool. It was old and musty. The previous occupants must have smoked inside for many years, the walls tinged yellow except where frames had once hung. Floral patterned carpet, which may once have been vibrant reds and greens, was grey and threadbare.

"It certainly has character," I commented, placing a box marked 'pots & pans' on a chipped tile kitchen countertop, "when was it built?"
"1904 according to the real estate agent. Thebarton is an old area. It's not much, I know."
"With a slap of paint it won't be bad, you might even have hardwood floors under the carpet if it's that old."

The carpet was at its worst by the open fireplace. Sparks and a rolling log or two had left burns, some as large as my hand. It was loose where the frayed edge met the stone hearth and we peeled it back to have a look. Beneath the carpet, the foam underlay had crumpled to yellow dust. Beneath that, the dark polished floorboards were lined with overlapping newspaper pages dating back to 1952.

"Jesus, they're actually really nice. You wouldn't even need to sand them. Do you want to rip the carpet out now before we bring in any furniture?"
"You'd help me do that?"
"Of course. It shouldn't take long and Seb and I didn't have anything planned for the rest of the day."
"I could order pizza delivery later..."
"That works."
"What if the floors are not all as nice as this?"
"They can't be worse than the carpet but we can peel up a few more areas to check if you like. Even if you do need to replace and stain-match a few boards, it'll be cheaper than replacing the carpet and will probably look amazing."
"Alright. I don't have a lot of money after, you know."
"Yes, I'm sure its been an interesting few months."
"A security guard. Can you believe that?"
"Where at?"
"I don't know, she wouldn't tell me. Which corner do you want to start at?"

The trapdoor was in the middle of the living room. It was large, almost five feet across, with heavy cast iron hinges and a round recessed handle. We'd discovered it when we removed the last of the carpet and swept the underlay and newspapers aside. All three of us gripped the heavy round handle and pulled.

"Can I go down?" asked Seb.
"Are you fucking kidding?" I asked, peering below. Wooden

steps disappeared into the darkness.

"It must be some kind of cellar," said my father, "I'll grab a flashlight. There's one in the back of the car."

Seb knelt at the edge while we waited for him to return.

"What do you reckon's down there?"

"Spiders."

"There's a switch on the wall a few steps down. I can just see it..." He laid flat and reached down.

"I wouldn't. Something will grab your arm."

Seb pulled his arm up quickly, "like what?"

"I dont know, some kind of demon or something."

"Some kind of demon?"

"Or something. Just wait for him to get back with the flashlight."

Seb reached down and flicked the switch.

A light came on downstairs, illuminating a bare concrete floor and pastel green walls. There were no spiders or demons. I tested the top step, it appeared solid. I did the same with the next. Seb bolted down past me. The room was large and empty but for a large metal door at one end. Seb rattled the handle.

"It's locked."

I've watched enough movies to know that when you come across a hidden cellar and it contains a locked metal door, it's probably locked for a reason and your best bet is to fuck off back up the stairs, close the trapdoor, and nail it down.

That wouldn't make for a very interesting story though so the people in the movies always discover a key or amulet that opens the door and then a demon or something tears them to pieces. Sometimes they will mix it up a bit and it's a verse read from an old book or a tune on a music-box that opens the door but the end result is always the same. If there had been a child's doll in the cellar I would have left right there and then.

"The hinges are on this side," said my father, "if we pry the pins out, we'll be able to take it straight off."
"Yes, but should we?"
"What are you talking about?"
"Never mind."
"Dad thinks there's a demon behind it."
"No I don't Seb, stop being stupid."
"Well if there is a demon, it's trespassing on my property. I'll grab a flathead screwdriver."
As my father made his way back up the stairs, Seb leaned towards me and whispered, "Do I call him Philip or Grandpa?"
"Whichever you prefer."
"Maybe Grandpa then. I'll see how it goes."
"You'll see how it goes?"
"Yes, I can always swap if it's strange. What do you really reckon is behind the door?"
"Another empty room probably."
"If it's empty, why would the door need to be locked?"
"Shut up Seb."

Philip returned with a screwdriver and pried the pins up and out of the hinges. The heavy door shifted a bit and Seb and I stepped back. I almost asked, "Shouldn't we all have some kind of weapon?" but censored myself in time. Wedging the screwdriver between the door and frame, Philip jimmied them apart a few inches. He shone the flashlight through the gap and then pulled the door fully open.

Beyond the doorway, lay a corridor. A long dark corridor. The beam from the flashlight barely reached the opposite end, two hundred feet or so away, where a metal ladder led up. Philip stepped through the doorway, shining the flashlight over the walls nearby and located a switch. Of the dozen or so lights strung along the corridor, three of them worked and it was more than enough light to make our way. We were silent as we approached the ladder and shone the flashlight up. Above us, was a trapdoor identical to the one in Philips living room.

"We can't just open it," I whispered, "we don't know what's on the other side."
"We didn't know what was on the other side of the metal door either," Philip replied, also whispering.
"Yes, but we're well past the property line of your place now. This is someone else's place. It might be someone else's living room. If I were sitting at home watching television and a trapdoor in the floor suddenly flew open, I'd have a heart attack."
"I could climb up and stick my ear against the trapdoor,"

suggested Seb, "if I hear a television we can just go back."
"Alright," I agreed, "just be careful."

Seb climbed the ladder until his head was bent against the trapdoor. I held my breath, I could hear Philip breathing deeply through his nose in the silence. Seb knocked loudly on the wood. "Hello?" he yelled.

"What the fuck, Seb?"
"I couldn't hear anything."
"Did I miss the bit of the plan where we all agreed you would bang and yell if you couldn't hear anything?"
"Should I try to lift it?"
"No."
Seb lifted the trapdoor. It was heavy and only moved a few inches before slamming back down.
"Oh my god Seb, climb back down or I'll sell you to the Gypsies."
"No, climb up here and help me. We can't just go back now without knowing what's up here."
"I can."
"Here, hold this," said Philip, handing me the flashlight and pulling himself up the rungs.
"Thanks Grandpa," Seb said, moving to the side to allow Philip room.
"No problem. On three."

On three, the trapdoor flew up, held at its apex for a brief moment, and slammed open with a resounding thud. Dust particles flooded the flashlight beam, diffusing its reach to a few feet beyond the hole.

"What's up there?"
"I don't know," replied Seb, " it's pretty dark. Pass me the flashlight."
I reached up and handed it to his outstretched hand, he swung back up and held the light above his head, flicking it back and forth.
"Oh my god," he said.
"You have to see this," said Philip.

It's annoying when you are watching a program and just at the exciting bit they cut to an advertisement. Unless it's that commercial for the Toyota Tundra with explosions and motor bikes doing jumps to the guy humming *The Ride of the Valkyries*. Everything is better with *The Ride of the Valkyries*. If you are not familiar with T*he Ride of the Valkyries*, it's the tune they play in the movie *Apocalypse Now* when the helicopters fly in to fuck things up. If at all possible, try to imagine *The Ride of the Valkyries* playing through the next few paragraphs as it will make them seem a lot more exciting and might even make up for the disappointing reveal after several pages of buildup.

I climbed the ladder and lifted myself over the edge, standing between Seb and Philip. The warehouse was huge, almost the size of a football field, dark but for a few slivers of light making their way through boarded up windows. Seb panned the light slowly across the wall to our right. A large mural had been painted, badly, of what appeared to be the dance floor from Saturday Night Fever fading into a city skyline at night. The city bit was a lot better than the dance floor bit but that's only because it's pretty hard to fuck up black rectangles and yellow dots. Really, they should have just done the whole thing as that. Or maybe just get someone in who knew what they were doing.

Seb shone the light to our left and up, following carpeted stairs to a glassed-in mezzanine. The words 'Snack Bar' were written in Bauhaus Bold behind a wood panelled counter, a poster above a vinyl booth advertised a coke and hotdog combo deal for 99 cents.

"99 cents for a coke and hotdog is pretty good," said Seb.
"Yes, but what is this place?" I asked.
He swung the flashlight to illuminate a carpeted area behind us. Behind a long dusty counter, rows of wooden shelves marked with numbers lay empty. A sign hanging above the shelves, also written in Bauhaus Bold, read 'Skate Hire'.
"It's a rollerskating rink," said Philip.

I did give a heads-up that it wasn't going to be a secret military base with a spaceship hidden under a tarpaulin. I told this story to my friend Geoffrey a few years back and just as I revealed that it was a warehouse, before getting to the rollerskating bit, he asked, "Was it full of porn?"
"What?"

"Was the warehouse full of boxes of porn?"
"No. It was a rollerskating rink."
"A what?"
"A rollerskating rink."
"Are you kidding? That's pretty lame. Were there people rollerskating?"
"What? No, it was an old abandoned rink. Why would people be rollerskating in the dark?"
"How would I know? I don't rollerskate. Nobody does. I thought it was going to be something exciting."
"And the most exciting thing you could imagine a warehouse containing is boxes of porn?"
"No, but I knew it wasn't going to be a spaceship."

Seb and I spent a lot of time at Philip's new house over the next few months. I think he looked forward to our visits. We helped paint the walls and arrange furniture but mainly we went there to skate. We'd discovered an electrical mains box in an alcove off the skate hire area. Many of the coloured spotlights above the skating rink had blown but there were enough to see by. Three or four faced a large centre mirrorball which splashed the area below with blue and green points of light. The fluorescent lights in the snack bar, bathrooms, and a DJ booth that overlooked the skating rink all worked.

Most of the sound equipment in the DJ booth was still there and operational. Seb tested a microphone and his voice flooded the skating floor. There were no records to play on the turntables but there was an old double-cassette player and a rack of cassettes with handwritten labels like *Sizzlin' Summer Hits 82* and *Sizzlin' Summer Hits 82 tape 2*.

A Coca-Cola branded glass door refrigerator in the snack bar hummed and lit up when we plugged it in. Seb found an apron with the words 'Thebarton Skate Arena' emblazoned across the front. He pretended to serve us from behind the counter when we later ordered pizza to the house and carried it through the corridor to eat in a vinyl booth. Philip pried open an old electronic cash register while we watched in anticipation but there was nothing in it.

There was a small kitchen off the snack bar with a chip-fryer and microwave. A box in one corner was full of skates and Seb and I searched through it for a pair that fit. They were stiff beige leather boots with thin orange plastic wheels that squeaked horribly as we rolled and stumbled awkwardly across the rink to Rod Stewart's *Young Turks* and the theme from *Chariots of Fire*.

Later, we bought rollerblades and became fairly proficient on them - not enough to claim gold if rolling in a circle was an Olympic event, but we could keep our balance and manage to stop. Eventually we were able to skate backwards for a bit and do small jumps. Another box we discovered in a bathroom cubicle was full of skating trophies and we presented them to each other whenever a particularly 'speccy' trick was performed. Philip didn't skate but he seemed to enjoy spending time in the DJ booth.

"And that was the Go-Go's again with their smash hit, *We Got The Beat*. Apparently it's every third song on this cassette. Coming up next, we have a little ditty 'bout two American kids named Jack and Diane…"

We didn't just use the warehouse to skate and listen to bad eighties music. We marked out tennis court lines using ducttape, raced remote-control cars, and played indoor cricket. Tennis and cricket proved difficult under rotating green and blue points of light so mostly we did just skate and listen to bad eighties music.

Back then, Seb was only with me every second weekend and a few nights between but we spent almost every hour of that time together at the warehouse. For nearly three months the Playstation was left off and toys ignored, our small concrete box in the city became just a place to sleep after getting back from 'Grandpa's House'. We became experts on which brand of oil was best for wheel bearings, which socks were least sweaty. Eighties mix tapes made their way into the car and Seb knew all of the lyrics by heart.

"What does 'never been to me' even mean?"
"I've no idea. It just sounds like she's having a bit of a brag. 'Poor me, I've been undressed by kings and seen some things, mainly in the mediterranean apparently, but I'm not sure who I really am. Please shower me with sympathy while I sip champagne on a boat.'"
"Maybe she has amnesia."

"Maybe. Or maybe she's just a self-absorbed cow. I mean, if I complained that I've jetted all over the world and rooted queens on boats but I'm not sure who the real David is, I'd be told to get over myself and stop being a prat."

"What do you reckon she saw?"

"Sorry?"

"The bit where she says she's seen some things that a woman ain't meant to see. What do you reckon it was?"

"Secret blueprints or something I suppose. She doesn't specifically say."

"Blueprints to what?"

"A tank or something."

"I think she's talking about a penis."

"Could be. It's a dreadful song regardless, fast forward it or put on *Tainted Love*."

"Where is it?"

"S*izzlin' Summer Hits 82 tape 5*. Song four, side two."

We thought of the rollerskating rink as ours. That it always would be. We had no idea what the warehouse had been used for prior to it being a skate rink, or why it was connected to Philip's house by an underground corridor, but it didn't matter. It had been boarded up and forgotten, and we had discovered it. It was ours to use however and whenever we wanted. Then it wasn't.

There was no reason for the trapdoor not to open. We had used it just the previous day. It never stuck and there was no lock. Philip and I climbed the ladder and put our shoulders into it together. It wouldn't move. We tried to jimmy it open with a tyre lever and hammer, even walked around the block looking for the boarded-over front entrance. Where we thought it should be were rows of townhouses. They didn't look all that old. Perhaps at the back of one of those townhouses was a courtyard with an old metal door the occupants had never opened. Perhaps it was covered by vines and forgotten. Perhaps we were just looking in the wrong place.

Seb and I rollerbladed at a nearby tennis court a few times after that but it wasn't the same. Joggers stopped to watch us and a tennis player told us off for leaving marks on the surface. Once when we were there, a group of teens threw pinecones at us, and when it rained we couldn't use it at all. Eventually we stopped going and when Seb grew out of his rollerblades, we didn't replace them.

We continued to visit Philip for a while but there wasn't much to do at his house. Our visits turned into short visits which became infrequent short visits. Philip watched the football or cricket while we were there. It's always either football or cricket season in Australia. Conversation, about cars and the weather, was kept to commercial breaks.

The last time we visited, Philip yelled at Seb for asking if we could try the trapdoor again. It would have meant moving a coffee table and rug again for no reason. Seb had a Playstation and toys at home and I had stuff to do.

It was a quick service. I said a few words about how much Philip loved football and cricket. Seb had chosen the song to play. The box lowered with a clank and whirr as *Centrefold* by the J. Geils Band (*Sizzlin' Summer Hits 82 tape 3*) played at a respectable level in the background.

Philip had never let on that he was sick. Or perhaps he had and I just didn't pick up on it. I vaguely recall him mentioning something about his prostate but I assumed that was something all old men deal with. To be honest, I'd thought he was talking about not being able to maintain an erection and had changed the subject.

There were only a handful of people at the crematorium, I didn't know any of them apart from my sister and I hadn't seen her in several years. She met Seb for the first time and invited us to visit sometime. I told her, "Okay, that sounds good."

The following weekend, while Seb and I were at Philip's house packing his belongings, we tried the trapdoor one last time. It wouldn't open but we thought we heard running and a shout above so maybe someone else had found a way in. Seb tried knocking but there was no answer.

We did visit my sister a few weeks later but there were no secret passageways in her house and neither Seb or I gave a fuck about her origami owls or potplant hangers. Any halfwit with a roll of string and a few sticks can set up an Etsy shop.

Romance

I proposed to Holly while we were playing tennis and she's never let me forget it. Maybe I should have written, "Holly will you marry me?" in tennis balls but I only had about five. Sorry I'm not a coach. If I could go back in time, I'd at least let her win the match. Whenever anyone describes the romantic situation in which they were proposed to, Holly gives me a pursed lip glance. It's gotten to the point where Holly actually blatantly lies about the proposal.

"And then, as Jeff and I watched the sun set in Bora Bora, the waiter brought me a piña colada and the ring was around the straw. How did David propose to you?"
"He wrote, "Holly, will you marry me?" in fireworks."
"Really?"
"Yes. And there was a band playing."
"Gosh, who?"
"The Beastie Boys."
"Oh my lord, where was it?"
"On the moon. David hired a rocket to take us all there. The fireworks people had to write, "Holly, will you marry me?" backwards because we were looking down at the Earth instead of up from it."
"You've been to the moon?"
"Yes, and the sun."

Love is Love

When I was eight, I had a relationship with one of my sister's dolls. It was a four-foot tall Snow White doll that looked a lot like a girl at my school named Emma Jenkins.

I never had sex with the doll but I kissed it a lot and told it that I loved it. I did almost consummate the relationship one afternoon, when my parents took my sister to a soccer match, but the other team forfeited and my parents returned early to discover us naked in bed.

I never saw Snow White again and I had to have 'the talk' that evening. My mother also borrowed a book from the library titled *What's Happening to Me? An Illustrated Guide to Puberty* and left it in my room with a sticky-note that said, "You're normal."

Relationships

There's a Japanese art called Kintsukuroi which consists of repairing broken bowls and dishes with lacquer mixed with powdered gold. As a philosophy, it treats breakage and repair as part of the history of an object, rather than something to disguise.

Some of the repaired bowls and dishes look nice and some turn out a bit dodgy. It depends on the degree of skill of course, whether the gold lacquer was slopped on with a brush or blended perfectly, but also on if the dish was worth repairing in the first place.

Some dishes are special dishes, like a limited edition Charles & Diana commemorative wedding dish, while other dishes are just dishes.

Our dishes get thrown out if they get chipped or broken, replaced when we realise we only have two left. There's no point wasting gold lacquer when we can get a Färgrik 18-piece dinnerware set from IKEA for $19.99.

Fast Clowns

I went to a friend's birthday party when I was five or six and there was a fast clown making balloon animals and hats. I asked the clown for a balloon hat and he made me a sausage dog. When I complained, he grabbed my arm really fast, squeezed hard enough to hurt, and said, "I don't give a fuck what you want kid, take the fucking sausage dog."

I intended to tell an adult but when I approached the birthday boy's mother, the clown appeared out of nowhere, grinned menacingly at me, and asked loudly, "Do you like your sausage dog?" and I replied, "Yes, thank you."

It was a long time ago but if I knew who that clown was and he was still working, I'd leave a bad review on Yelp. I think his name was Barry.

Medieval Society

I attended a medieval society gathering once, but only because my friend Geoffrey needed a lift. People who participate in medieval gatherings don't tend to own vehicles. I sat in my car the entire time to avoid being asked, "Whateth is this strange garb thou weareth?"

Adding 'eth' to the end of a word doesn't make it medieval, it makes it stupid. After about an hour of watching Geoffrey leap out from behind trees and whack people with his sword, I wound down the window and yelled, "How long are you going to be Geoffrey?" and he yelled back, "That's *Sir* Geoffrey, my goodeth fellow."

I'm fairly certain nobody in mediaeval times said the word 'goodeth' and there is no way Geoffrey would have been a knight if he'd been born in mediaeval times. He'd be the one being whacked by knights for not growing enough potatoes and making up words. After a hard day's work and several whackings, he'd lay down in the soil, cover himself with straw, and go to sleep imagining all the things he would do to the knights if he were a wizard.

Girls Named Louise

Louise is a fat girl's name and horrible to say. It's almost as bad as the name Gwyneth. Both sound like they are being squeezed out of a balloon.

I went to school with a girl named Louise. She was a huge heifer with tight curly hair and a moustache. Once during a school game of soccer, she ran to the edge of the playing field, dropped her shorts, and did a poo. This is the kind of thing people named Louise do. The gym teacher had to pick it up with a plastic shopping bag.

I also knew a Gwyneth once. She was bi-polar and stabbed her boyfriend Stuart in the arm with a steak-knife during an argument about electric cars. It was the second worst dinner party I have ever been to.

The worst dinner party I have ever been to was when Gwyneth and Stuart held another six months later and I was the only person who showed up. I made a joke about swapping the cutlery with plastic utensils and Gwyneth cried.

Wills

I've never been bequeathed anything in a will. I've seen television shows and movies where family members dressed in black are sitting in a lawyer's office listening in anticipation as a will is read, but they're generally families that have money. Someone gets bequeathed a house and a million dollars and someone scowls and says they'll fight it in court. A will reading for anyone in our family would sound like someone who works at Goodwill listing off the contents of a box left at the back door.

"And to David, I bequeath my four-slice toaster, eight teaspoons, and a fitted sheet."

The closest I've ever come to inheriting something is when my father died and I found a George Foreman grill and two large boxes of pornography in his shed. It wasn't even good pornography, mostly Playboy and VHS cassettes with titles like *New Wave Hookers* and *Massage Parlour Wives*. I didn't even bother watching them, which says a lot as I once masturbated to an episode of *20/20*. At the bottom of one of the boxes, there was an envelope and an inflatable sex doll. The envelope contained Polaroid Instamatic photos, which I burned, and the sex doll was brittle and cracked where it had been folded. The vagina bit still worked though.

Fondue

When I was growing up, my parent's friends were mostly people they knew from their local tennis club. They were all very polite and well dressed and sometimes we had parties at our place where everyone would stand around eating fondue while Boney-M albums played in the background at a level that wouldn't hinder conversation.

"Fantastic fondue guys, what kind of cheese do you use?"
"Kraft."
"Delicious. I also love this album. Boney M are going to be the next Beatles. You mark my words. Have you heard the track, *Ra Ra Rasputin?*"
"Yes, fantastic isn't it? It's just called *Rasputin* though."
"Is it?"
"Yes. They sing Ra Ra Rasputin in the song but it's just called *Rasputin.*"
"Well there you go. I did not know that."

Coloured Things

There were games in our house when I was growing up but none of them were board games. They were games my parents made me play when I said I was bored. In summer, my father would say, "Only boring people get bored, go outside and run around in the sprinkler."

In winter, it would be the bit about boring people followed with, "Why don't you blow up a balloon and tap it around the house making sure it doesn't touch the ground?"
We must have been poor because other kids had Atari. Now that I think about it, our car was pretty crap as well.

I've played board games since and am not a big fan. They take ages to set up and put away and the bit between isn't exactly a day at a water park. I used a water park as a 'fun comparison' because my partner Holly dragged me to one recently called *Wet'n'Wild* and, despite my reservations, I had fun. It was wet and relatively wild - it depends what scale you're using I suppose. If the scale ranged from 'using a different coffee mug than your favourite one' to 'bringing down a wild boar with only a knife', it wouldn't rate all that highly. Probably a sixteen. We paid extra for plastic wristbands that allowed us to skip queues, and walking past others to the front of the line all day was the best part. It's probably how the Kardashians feel all of the time.

Out of all the board games I have played, Trivial Pursuit is, by far, the worst. Firstly, I don't care if the bits are called pies or cheeses, everything's a thing. Just move my thing for me and give me a coloured thing if I get the answer right. Secondly, everything else. The game takes fifteen days to play. By the thirty-eighth consecutive hour of gameplay I just want someone to win, I don't care who.

"Okay, geography, what country has kangaroos?"
"Really, David? That's the question?"
"Yes."
"Australia."
"Well done. Have a blue thing."
"I'm not on a category space, it wasn't for a cheese wedge."
"Have a blue thing anyway."
"Give me a look at the card."
"Why?"
"Just give me a look."
"Fine."
"The question was, 'The Kalinigrad Oblast borders which body of water?'"
"Mine was a bonus question."
"Right, I'm not playing if you are going to reverse cheat. It's a waste of everyone's time."
"So you forfeit?"
"No, do you forfeit?"
"Yes."
"Fine. Loser has to pack up the game. Make sure all the cards are facing the right way for next time."

There's practically nothing I wouldn't rather do than play Trivial Pursuit... that may be a bit of stretch as I'd obviously prefer to play Trivial Pursuit than spend the night in a spider cave, but you get the point. I'd choose giving Holly a foot massage over playing Trivial Pursuit and I've no desire to go through all the prep, effort, mess and cleanup of moisturiser based activities unless I'm home alone. I know it's not meant to be a chore but neither is hugging after sex or remembering birthdays. Call me selfish, I can't hear you - my home office is lined with egg-cartons to block the sound of my neighbour Carl's mower.

Holly, on the other hand, grew up playing board games. The bookshelf at her parent's house is stacked with dozens of them, everything from Boggle to Trouble... I was going for an A to Z thing there but I couldn't think of any board games that start with A and the only game I could think of that started with a letter after T was Yahtzee, which isn't a board game. Neither are Boggle or Trouble really... The bookshelf at Holly's parent's house is stacked with board games, everything from checkers to Trivial Pursuit - which is Holly's favourite board game. There are other things on her parent's bookshelf of course, a knitted rooster, books about cats, photos of Holly with ex-boyfriends. I'm not the jealous type but sometimes I'll point and ask, "do you ever wonder what your life would be like if you stayed with this potato-headed zit factory with facial hair that looks like a mediaeval Scottish woman's crotch? No? I bet you do. You still love him don't you? Are you Facebook friends?"

Being Holly's favourite game, our bookshelf at home contains five copies of Trivial Pursuit, including a beat up original Genus edition, a 10th Anniversary edition, a Family edition, a *Star Wars* Collector's edition, a 20th Anniversary edition and a Welcome to America edition. They're all equally as horrid to play, even the *Star Wars* one. You'd think it would be better than the others but it isn't; nobody knows Lando Calrissian's home address or what planet produced the thread that Ben Skywalker's underpants are woven from and the type of person who might doesn't have any friends to play Trivial Pursuit with. I love Star Wars as much as the next person, don't get me wrong, I just have better things to do than learn to speak Wookiee. I wouldn't mind a stormtrooper outfit though. I'm not sure what for but it would be good to have. Even if just to wear around the house and while doing yard work. I wouldn't wear it out though, not unless it was 501st Legion certified.

The last time I played Trivial Pursuit, over Christmas with Holly's parents and her brother, I honestly thought I was going to die. On several occasions, while I waited the four hours for my next roll of the dice, my eyes rolled back in my head and I felt my body just giving up. When Holly's brother won his final thing, and the game, I almost wept with relief. As I began to pack up, Holly's father stopped me and said, "No, we play on to see who comes second."

Scriptwriters

We only had one televison channel in the small town I lived in as a child. It ran from 3PM to 11PM and showed loops of *MASH*, *Lost in Space*, and *Gentle Ben*. For those unfamiliar with *Gentle Ben*, it was *Flipper* but with a bear. All I recall of the series is that a boy's father rode through a marsh on a boat with a giant propeller on the back, and a bear always saved the day by tugging a rope. It wouldn't matter what the issue was, a bank robbery or a bomb, the bear, which I think was named Ben, tugged a rope. The boy would then make a rope related pun such as, "Guess they got roped into that one," and the father would laugh and tussle the boy's hair. Apart from coming up with a different rope pun each week, working on the script must have been a pretty cushy job.

"Right, episode 82, there's a cattle stampede and the bear tugs a rope and saves the day."
"But it doesn't make any sense. Why are cattle stampeding in a marsh and how would tugging a rope stop them?"
"You're overthinking it, Greg, just work on the rope pun."
"Fine. How about, 'well he sure roped them in'?"
"Didn't we use that in the episode where the bear saved the school bus from going over a cliff by tugging on a rope?"
"No, that was, 'Ropey ropey rope rope'."
"Ah yes, not one of your best."

Didits

As an Australian who learned the metric system in school, the only way I can calculate weight in the United States using the imperial system is to compare it to common objects. I know eighty pounds is a big bag of concrete so I just base everything off that: Forty pounds is half a big bag of concrete, ten pounds is a cat, twenty pounds is two cats, and a tractor with a backhoe attachment is more than my vehicle can tow.

I have no idea who came up with the imperial system but I would have liked to have been there when the idea was pitched.

"Look, it's simple. Three barleycorns is an inch, twelve inches is a foot, three feet is a yard, twenty-two yards is a chain, ten chains is a furlong, eight furlongs is a mile, and three miles is a league."
"It's a bit all over the place."
"No it isn't."
"How am I meant to remember all those different numbers?"
"You're not, it's impossible. Just remember the first few."
"What if someone needs to measure something smaller than a barleycorn?"

"That's the beauty of the inch, it's divided into sixteenths."
"Right. And what are those increments called?"
"One sixteenth of an inch."
"Or one fifth and a third of a barleycorn?"
"Why are you trying to make this more difficult than it is?"
"I'm not, I'm just trying to wrap my head around it. Explain the weight thing again."
"Okay, twenty-seven grains is a scruple, three scruples is a dram, fifteen drams is an ounce, sixteen ounces is a pound, fourteen pounds are a stone, and one-hundred and forty-three stone is a ton."
You're just making it all up as you go along, aren't you?"
"No."
"I'm fairly sure you said boople the first time, not scruple."
"No, I didn't."

My offspring and I built a deck recently. We estimated the project would take two weeks and cost one thousand dollars to finish. I took six months and just under twelve grand. The time blowout can partly be attributed to the fact that the original plans kept changing, and partly due to our construction experience consisting entirely of watching time-lapse videos on YouTube.

"We're adding a koi pond?"
"Yes, incorporated into the deck."
"How much extra time will that add to the construction?"
"Eight minutes and sixteen seconds."

I use the word 'plans' loosely of course. There were no blueprints that some professional architect spent months tweaking. No project manager on site unrolling said blueprints and giving a little nod then pointing at things. The plans were drawn on the back of Comcast bill with a Sharpie, and included measurements such as 'twelve and a half big steps' and 'four metal frogs and a didit'. The actual length of a 'didit' was never defined but became a standard throughout the project.

"How long does this piece of wood need to be, Seb?"
"Three crusty work gloves and a didit."
"Long didit or short didit?"
"Standard didit."

Using inches wasn't an option because neither Seb or I could work out how to read the measuring tape.

"It's... four feet, six and three-quarter inches, and a tenth and one sixth of a barleycorn."
"What?"
"I'll just make a mark on the measuring tape with a Sharpie."

Monkey-Bar Intel

I've only ever cheated on someone once in my life. I was eight and I wasn't aware that Morgan Nelson and I were dating when I circled *Yes* on a note asking *Do you like Emma?*

Morgan and I had ridden our bikes part of the way home together the day before so it's possible something was said that I missed or she misinterpreted. Maybe she was just impressed by my bunny-hops. According to relayed monkey-bar intel, Emma didn't actually like me at all. The note had been a test, which I'd failed, and Morgan and Emma were planning to wait for me outside the front school gates after class and beat me up. As Morgan was a bit of a heifer and Emma took Karate lessons, there was a very real possibility of being hurt so I stayed late after class and left through the back gates. The next day, my explanation of staying late to research caterpillars for a school report was declared a weak excuse and I was accused of being too scared to fight girls - which I vehemently denied to the point of declaring I'd fight five girls at once.

They were waiting for me at the bike racks after the bell rang - five girls and several spectators, - but I was prepared. At lunchtime, I'd emptied out my drinking bottle and filled it with piss.

Bin

I heard Jodie fart this morning. I actually heard her fart three times - four if you count the little squeak at the end as she made a final check.

She hadn't seen me when she walked upstairs and sat at her desk - I was under mine plugging in my laptop cable. I popped my head up when I heard the first fart, it was like one of those fake ones you make by licking your arm and giving it a raspberry, one with a lot of spit. Her back was to me and I watched as she lifted her left cheek and farted again. The first must have been a test run because the second ran for triple the time and at a much lower pitch. It was like a drawn out sigh mixed with the sound of a flag flapping in a strong breeze. The third was shorter, softer, and faded out like a librarian saying 'shhhhh'. The fourth, as mentioned, was just a small squeak - or like that water-drop noise some people can make by flicking their cheek.

At the sound of someone walking up the stairs, Jodie quickly wafted the air behind her with a hand. Mike stepped off the landing and made a face.
"Jesus fucking Christ, what's that smell?" he asked.
"I know," Jodie replied, nodding and making a distasteful face, "I smelled it when I came up. I think it's David's bin."

Mammoths

Four years ago, my partner Holly asked me to laminate a news clipping about a cat that had adopted a mouse. Inserting the clipping, which featured a photo of a cat and mouse sleeping in a basket with the caption 'Purrfect Parenting', it came out the other end with a dead fly between the layers. Apparently I had done this on purpose.

On Monday morning, I walked into the kitchen to find Holly making toast. I generally feel safe eating toast that Holly has made because it requires minimal ingredients to forget, replace, or experiment with, but this toast was a bit thin and soggy.

"It's a bit thin and soggy," I said, "what bread is this?"
"It's the same bread we always have," Holly replied, pointing to the bag.
"I didn't even know we had any brea...oh my god," I exclaimed, "it has a best-before date of January 2009."
"It was in the freezer," Holly said defensively, "The best before date doesn't count if the product is frozen."
"I'm fairly sure there's a limit." I held up a slice of bread consisting almost entirely of permafrost.
"No there isn't," Holly replied, "I saw a show once where scientists found a Mammoth frozen in ice for millions of

years. They thawed it out, cooked it and ate it. "

"That didn't happen, you told me once that you saw a show about a man who ate his own head and it turned out to be an animated gif. Why would scientists eat a mammoth?"

"Because they're scientists, and they know a lot more about science and how long things can be frozen for and still be eaten than you do. You don't even know how to use a laminating machine."

Staring as Holly raised a thin soggy piece of toast to her mouth and took a bite, she chewed and added thoughtfully, "I like mammoths. I wish we had one. A small one, for the dog to play with."

Baby Birds

I watched a boy named Raymond kill a nest of baby birds when I was eleven. He was older than me, by three or four years, the brother of a boy in my class. I don't remember that classmate's name or why I'd ridden with him to his house after school but I remember Raymond calling us into the backyard. There were four baby birds in the nest, eyes barely open but strong enough to raise their beaks and make a ruckus. Perhaps they thought they were about to be fed. An adult bird, a sparrow I think, hopped from branch to branch above us making angry noises. Raymond held the nest in one hand and smiled. He held a tennis racquet in his other hand.

Afterwards, as I was riding my bike home, I began to cry. Not because of what *he'd* done, but because I hadn't tried to stop him. Because I'd stood there watching him throw the nest into the air and swing at it, watched him pick up a baby bird he'd missed and throw that into the air and swing again. I cried because when he'd laughed, I'd feared the repercussion of doing or saying anything that showed disapproval, and I laughed as well. I stopped my bike, put my head on my handlebars and sobbed, replaying my laugh over and over in my mind. There was a rock, slightly larger than my fist, laying by the side of the road. I picked it up and turned my bike around.

Raymond answered the door when I knocked. There was only a few feet between us and I threw the rock as hard as I could. There was a lot of anger in my throw, at him and myself. Blood splattered my face and the door as he went backwards onto the floor. For a moment he was still and I thought he was dead, then he gurgled, spat blood onto his cheeks, and groaned. I turned, picked up my bike, and rode home.

I was in bed when the police arrived. It must have taken them some time to get my information from the school registry. My mother was away with my sister at the time, chaperoning a school trip; my father answered the door and invited them in. He knew why they were there as I'd arrived home splattered in blood. I put a dressing gown on over my pyjamas and sat on the edge of the bed, waiting for the police to walk down the hall, open my door, and take me to jail.

Later, my father said that he had told the officers how Raymond had killed the baby birds and that I had tried to stop him and had been threatened with the tennis racquet. The damage to Raymond's face hadn't been as bad as it looked, a busted nose and lip. The police put it down to boys being boys and chose not to file charges. I should have been pleased about that I suppose, relieved at least, but it hadn't been boys being boys, it was the day I realised how weak and fearful I was, how I'd conformed, given approval to cruelty to protect myself. My father's lie was who I should have been, not who I was.

I was riding home from school a few weeks later when I heard a shout behind me. Looking back, I saw Raymond and three other boys around his age riding their bikes after me. Perhaps I should have ridden faster, attempted to escape, but instead, I stopped. They broke my bike, one of the boys kicked it over and jumped on the spokes. I was kicked from behind and went down, kicked again in the shoulder, my collarbone snapped. I heard ringing, a kick to an ear, to my testicles, to my teeth. The beating was severe, but quick. It was less than a few minutes before Raymond and the boys got back on their bikes and rode off.

There was a bus stop shelter no more than thirty feet away and from it, an old man, perhaps in his sixties, had watched the beating in silence. He walked over and held out a hand.
"Are you okay?" he asked.
I winced as he helped me up.
"I would have done something but... I thought..."
I nodded.

Perhaps he'd chided himself afterwards, played out preferred scenarios in his head. Or maybe a lifetime of self-preservation had made it the norm, the obvious and only choice. I wheeled my bike home and told my parents I had lost control on a steep hill. I had to wear a sling and eat puréed bananas for a few months but my collarbone mended and my front teeth were replaced. I wasn't able to ride while my arm was healing and I was on a bus the last time I ever saw Raymond.

It was a couple of months after the beating and I was on my way to school. The bus pulled up at a stop for someone to alight and, from my window at the back, I saw Raymond on the sidewalk below. He was sitting on his bike, a foot or so from the curb and several feet ahead of me, smoking a cigarette and talking to a girl. He was facing away and hadn't noticed me. I waited until the door sighed closed and the engine revved before opening my window. As Raymond passed below, I reached out and grabbed his hair.

A nicer ending to this story might have been if I'd encountered a group of bullies picking on a small child or throwing rocks at a kitten, and, putting my own safety aside, chose to stand up to injustice. Or perhaps rescuing Raymond himself from bullies, or quicksand, and becoming friends in the end. That's not how things work though and kids are assholes.

I managed to hold on for almost two blocks before I lost my grip. The bus was doing perhaps forty or forty-five miles per hour at that stage and I watched out the back window as Raymond rolled and bounced along the road. He covered a fair distance. I closed the window and smiled.

Alpha-Crotinials

I know an elderly woman named Sarah who dresses like a sixteen-year-old. She was at a function Holly and I attended recently and she said to Holly, "We should have a girls night out some time!" I agreed that it was a great idea because Holly has never played Bingo.

Apparently Sarah is only thirty-nine but she's been thirty-nine for thirty years and has two children, also in their thirties. I tell everyone I'm sixty because I'd much rather have people asking what my secret to younger looking skin is than thinking, "So that's what happens when you smoke a pack a day and only drink coffee for forty-odd years."

"Damn, you don't look sixty, David. What's your secret to younger looking skin?"
"Dryer lint and mayonnaise."
"What?"
"A one-to-one ratio. I mix it together well in a blender and wear it as a mask for ten minutes. The micropolyamides in the lint activate the alpha-crotinials in the mayonnaise, which super-hydrates the top six layers of derma."
"Really?"
"Yes, you should try it."
"I will."

Ben's Shirt

My coworker Ben bought a new shirt on the weekend. He wore it to work Monday and flitted gaily in and out of people's offices all morning for us to admire. It looked like any other shirt, perhaps a little shinier because of the cotton/nylon blend, but it wasn't like any other shirt; it was the best shirt in the world. It hadn't been advertised as such but Ben had suspected the shirt was the best shirt in the world the moment he saw it in on the rack. When he tried it on in the changing room, he knew it was. The points on the collar were extra sharp and the collar itself was slightly lower than usual. It also had the second to top button in the correct place; not so high that it looked silly when done up and not so low that it showed chest hair when left undone. It was light blue, bordering on grey-blue. The kind of grey-blue that looks great with either a suit or jeans. He'd worn it tucked in that day but it looked equally as good untucked, it was the perfect length for either. Ninety-five dollars was expensive for a shirt but not for the best shirt in the world. Besides, he'd received ten percent off for signing up for a department store credit card.

"New shirt?" asked Mike.
"Yes," replied Ben, beaming, "it's John Varvatos."
"It's very shiny. You look like you're on your way to a disco."

Hedgehogs

I've never really been much into drugs. I smoke marijuana from time to time (8am to 11pm) and I've tried practically everything else once, but the fear of making a spectacle of myself in public has always overridden the fun of being high.

Perhaps I should just 'loosen up a bit', as has been suggested, and inject heroin into my eyeballs, but at this point in my life I'd rather spend the money on plants.

"Okay, well I'm off. Have a good weekend, David."
"You too. Anything exciting planned?"
"Yes, I'm attending a rave in a forest. The only way to get there is by ATV but Bassnectar is playing so it should be worth the two-hour ride. I'm going to take a lot of drugs and have sex with girls wearing furry boots. Yourself?"
"I'm going to plant a birch."
"Nice."
"Yes, I'm a big fan of the birch."

I met a heroin addict once. It's possible I've met others and didn't realize because they were 'high-functioning' addicts, but the one I met was one of the barely-functioning ones. Her name was Simone and she was in her early twenties but looked a lot older - like a blonde Iggy Pop - and would have needed to run around in the shower to get wet. I was nineteen and had invited a handful of people over for a house-warming party after moving into a new apartment. Twenty or so people came and went that night, mostly friends of friends, many of which I'd never met. Simone was one of them and she had her four-year-old son with her.

The toddler sat quietly playing *Sonic the Hedgehog* on my Sega Mega Drive for most of the night, but was curled up on the sofa asleep when Simone left. There was no mention about looking after the child, or indication when she was coming back, she just left him. Like someone might leave a packet of cigarettes or sunglasses behind.

Around midnight, after everyone had left, I draped a blanket over the child and went to bed. In the morning, I made him toast and we played video games. His name was Jacob and he liked *Thomas the Tank Engine*. There was still no sign of his mother by mid-morning so I called around and one of the friends of a friend knew the street Simone lived on, but not the house number.

I stacked a couple of pillows on the passenger seat of my car, buckled Jacob in, and drove to the street he lived on. We agreed, during the drive, that hedgehogs aren't blue in real life. I'm not sure why that's memorable. He was very astute for a four-year-old and pointed out his house and his mother's car when we drove slowly down the street. I pulled into the driveway behind a rusty Honda Civic hatchback with a faded yellow 'Baby on board' sign suction-capped to the back window. There was a plastic playset in the front yard, with steps to a small slippery-dip and turnable blocks of tic-tac-toe. The colours were bleached by the sun and one of the tic-tac-toe blocks was missing. The slippery dip part had a large crack in it and was lying several feet away from the playset in long grass.

An upstairs window was open and I could hear music but there was no answer when I knocked on the door. Jacob reached up on tippy toes and turned the handle to let himself in. I followed him into the living room and shouted up the stairs. There was no reply.

"She's in the bath," Jacob told me, "She listens to music when she's having a bath and I have to stay downstairs and be good."

I stayed with him for about fifteen minutes - watched as he pottered about picking up trash and emptying ashtrays. There was a potted plant on top of an old Teac television set that may have once been a Ficus. Three Christmas tree decorations hung from the dead branches - two silver balls and a Sydney Opera House fridge magnet with string taped to it - even though it was nowhere near Christmas. The couch, salmon velour, had seen better days. Better decades really. The arms were torn and the underlying foam was dry and brittle. The style was like something you'd buy from Shewel's. There was no other furniture.

At one point Jacob disappeared into the kitchen and I heard running water so looked in. He'd pulled a chair over to the counter, climbed up on it, and was washing the dishes in the sink. When he was done, he took a cloth and crawled over the countertops, wiping them down. I asked if he was going to be okay and he nodded. I asked if he needed anything and he shook his head.

I dropped the Sega Mega Drive and my collection of games off at Jacob's house a few days later. I didn't really play it much. The upstairs window was open and I could hear music, but nobody answered when I knocked so I left it on the porch.

HOA

It snows where we live. Not by Alaskan standards of course, but enough to need a vehicle that can make it up and down slippery roads between December and March. As we live in a rural area, without state-maintained roads, an old man named Doug clears the snow whenever he fucking feels like it. Or not at all.

I guess Doug figures that if the forecast calls for snowfall all week, why not wait and do it all at once? I'm not exactly sure what our HOA fee covers - probably the fifty or so inflatable Christmas decorations he adds to his front yard around this time. It helps to think of the penguin inside a snowglobe and the waving snowman as our contribution to the neighborhood festivities. Nobody around here is caroling or swapping boiled puddings.

We received a request from Doug a while back for an additional $250 to fix a pothole and it turned out it was in his driveway. I'm fairly sure that's not how it works but a conversation with Doug lasts around four hours so we just sent the cheque.

Before I knew better, when we hadn't been here more than a season, I had a two hour conversation with Doug on the street about a bear he once saw walk across his front lawn. Then he repeated the story as if he hadn't just told it. It wasn't a robot bear or a bear wearing pants. There was no wrestling or fending off the bear with a sharp stick. A bear just walked across his lawn.

A conversation regarding a bear walking across your lawn should consist of 1. the fact, 2. possibly a small amount of exaggeration for entertainment purposes, and 3. maybe a sign-off such as, "So there you go," or, if you really need to retell the adventure, "So there you go, a bear walked across my lawn."

"I saw a bear walk across my front lawn once."
"Really?"
"Yes. A big one. So there you go, a bear walked across my lawn."

I just used the stopwatch on my phone to time how long it took to read that and, even allowing for a bit of nodding and pointing to get into character, it took just under twelve seconds. So there you go, my neighbour Doug once took two and a half hours to tell me that he saw a bear walk across his front lawn.

Jason Statham

My offspring Seb and I purchased a 44-gallon drum from a guy on Craigslist last autumn. We drilled a dozen or so holes in the side, packed it with dead leaves, and, after instructing Seb to add a splash of fuel from a jerry can, I went inside to get a lighter.

"How much fuel did you put in?"
"A splash."
"The jerry-can is empty."
"A decent splash."

I expected a 'whoompf' but I didn't expect the volume, or for the drum to act like a cannon. Burning leaves shot high into the air and rained down over a four hundred foot radius. There was a fair amount of screaming and running. Seb lost a new t-shirt to a burn hole, which he was rather upset about, but I refused to drive him to the mall to replace it.

"We have to go, Pacsun will sell out of these shirts and I'll never find another one with pineapples on the pocket."
"You should have thought about that before dumping several gallons of fuel into the 44-gallon drum. I'm not leaving the house for four or five weeks."
"Oh my god, Dad, it's not even that noticeable. Just draw on

eyebrows with a marker and wear a hat."
"Yes, that's an excellent suggestion, Seb. Perhaps a snappy vest and a cane to complete the ensemble."
"Your hair's not even that bad. Just short at the front."
"I have *no* hair at the front. It's just little frizzle-balls. I look like an old Chinese man that works on a wharf. All I need is a couple of big sacks on my back."
"Shave it all off then. You'll look like Jason Statham."
"You really think so?"
"...Sure."

The problem is that some people's heads are Jason Statham shaped and others are concentration camp prisoner shaped. You never really know what shape your head is, or how white, until you go #0 with a set of Wahl dog grooming clippers. I'd watched a movie a few nights before, called *The Descent*, about a group of women who go spelunking without spare flashlight batteries and get chased by pale, bald humanoid creatures that live in the dark. I watched it by myself and there were a lot of jump scares, which explains why, for two or three days after shaving my head, I'd yell and go all wobbly whenever I passed a mirror.

"I don't look anything like Jason Statham."
"Yes, you do. If he had no muscles and was maybe sick or something."
"If he was sick?"
"Cancer or something. Can we go to Pacsun now?"

Later, we learned our neighbor Carl had recorded the entire 'rain of fire' incident on his phone and presented the video during that week's sub-division HOA meeting. Apparently it's against the rules to burn rubbish in your backyard because a horse burnt to death in 1876. The fine is a shiny shilling or forfeiture of your least-unattractive daughter to the town's elders. There are also ordinances covering pitching your neighbor's well, rolling your sleeves above the elbow while churning butter, and, for the record, mowing your lawn after 7pm and before 9am. Also, nobody's allowed to own chickens.

Conveniently, Carl is the president of our sub-division HOA and there are only two other members: Carl's short, round, curly-haired wife Toni, who seconds every motion, and Janice Roberts, a 93 year-old semi-mobile corpse from across the street who owns chickens and has a large sign in her front yard that states, *Though I may stumble, I will not fall, for the Lord upholds me with his hand. Psalms 37:23.* Which is false, as I've seen Janice fall at least three times. Despite a decade or two of using a walker, it's as though each outing is the first time she's ever seen one; there's no 'lift, place, step, repeat' rhythm, its just random flailing and clanking. I saw her using it upside down once, she was holding onto the tennis balls. On one occasion, she somehow managed to throw the walker twenty feet ahead, fell, and couldn't get up for several minutes. I would have eventually helped but a UPS driver stopped and lifted her off the road before I finished my coffee.

According to the written warning I received - signed, countersigned and witnessed by Carl, Toni and Janice - it was the sixth recorded instance of Seb and I breaking HOA ordinances. Some of Carl's earlier work included, *Thorne's riding ATVs on the road*, *Thorne's feeding raccoons*, and, my personal favourite, *Thorne's rolling a log down a hill into a creek*.

I emailed the HOA my own video footage (an animated gif titled *Carl_sucking_horse_cock*) but they didn't respond.

TJ Maxx

There's a TJ Maxx in the same plaza as the supermarket where Holly and I shop. Sometimes Holly suggests popping in to have a quick look and I sigh and say, "Oh, okay then," but really I'm quite pleased. While Holly browses, I head straight to the soaps and give each a good sniff.

By the time Holly's done, with a trolley full of cushions, photo frames and designer dog toys, I'll usually have thirty soaps in a 'we're definitely getting these' pile and another ten or fifteen in a 'smell this, what do you think?' pile. There's a third pile but that's just a 'I don't want this but check out the packaging' stack. We have an entire cupboard full of soaps at home. Sometimes I stand in front of it and open and close the door really fast several times so I'm fanned by the combined scents.

Actually, I've only done that once or twice, I usually have much better things to do. I don'tt want to give the impression that I just stand around at home wafting the smell of soap towards myself. I spend far more time watching television and yelling at the dogs. I also read sometimes and we have a meth-lab in the basement. That Pepsi aint eight-balling itself.

The Recipent Incident

A few years back, our secretary Sharon resigned after what is now commonly referred to as The Recipent Incident.

Mistakenly selecting 'Staff' instead of her boyfriend 'Steve', Sharon sent a selfie of herself wearing only pigtails to everyone in the office. Being fat - or 'curvy' as fat people prefer to be called - the thing that impressed me most about the selfie was her flexibility. There's no way I could get my feet behind my head, even with a pillow under my back like she had. I've tried.

While I can understand Sharon's decision to leave without notice, the subject matter was actually less embarrassing than the environment the photo was taken in. Her bedroom had green striped wallpaper and a ruffled floral bedspread. A stained glass lamp shaped like a butterfly was just visible amongst a throng of teddy bears on her side table and, above her bed, was a poster of a tiger.

Who lives like this? If it was my bedroom, I wouldn't be taking nude selfies, I would be weeping as I splashed kerosene about and lit a match.

Kombucha

I'd never heard of kombucha until Holly bought a DIY kit and turned our kitchen into a laboratory. For three weeks, a huge jellyfish-shaped blob of bacteria sat fermenting in a five-gallon jug of tea on our countertop. Even just looking at the blob made me feel ill - the one time I had a curious sniff, I dry-retched for about three minutes and had to lie down.

Tasting the terrifying slop wasn't by choice; Holly made tacos one night and added a hot sauce she'd ordered online called Da Bomb Beyond Insanity. I'm not sure what the Scoville rating of the sauce is, I doubt Mr Scoville even had this kind of bullshit in mind when he came up with the chart. I've been on actual fire before and that was nowhere near as painful. This was like being kicked in the face by a horse made out of fire-ants and the worst thing I'd ever put in my mouth - up until I grabbed Holly's glass of what I thought was apple juice and threw it back.

It's impossible to describe the taste of Holly's homemade kombucha, it was all the tastes, but a blend of vinegar, fish, whiteboard cleaner, brake fluid, and magnets comes close.

"I'm going blind."
"Please, you're overreacting a bit."

"It's the worst thing I've ever tasted and I once ate a moth. My face is melting and now I've been poisoned."
"Here, drink this glass of milk, it'll cool your mouth."
"Did you use the same glass the kombucha was in?"
"I rinsed it first."
"No you didn't."
"How can you tell?"
"The milk's curdled. It's like a sloppy cheese."

I caught Holly pouring the jug of kombucha down the sink a few hours later. I nodded and said, "Pretty bad, huh?" and she replied, "No, it was quite good but I found a dead millipede in the jug. I'll cover it with cheesecloth next time."

Also, before Holly poured the jug down the sink, she took a photo and posted it on Facebook with the hashtags #firsttryatkombucha #turnedoutamazing #yum. Someone commented, "You'll have to give me the recipe!" so I replied with, "Do you have any millipedes?" and Holly deleted my comment and yelled at me.

Paintball

A few years back, my coworker Simon convinced me to play paintball. It was for his nephew's birthday and they needed to make up the numbers required for a team. I met Simon at the venue and he introduced me to his teenage nephew, four of the nephew's gaming friends, and his girlfriend Cathy - a short chubby gothic with only one hand.

I'd seen a photo of her and Simon but they'd had their arms around each other so the stump wasn't evident. I learned later she'd lost the hand as a child in an Insinkerator accident which is pretty much the worst way I can image losing a hand... actually, I thought about it and came up with several worse ways but most involved spider eggs hatching so I thought it best not to list them here.

Cathy still had a nub, and a smaller nub on that which was half a thumb, but it wasn't much use due to tendon and nerve damage. To be honest, it would have been a lot less creepy if she'd just lost the whole thing and worn a rubber hand or something. I shook the nub when I met her without shuddering, which I feel was pretty mature and accepting of me. It was squishy like a sausage. She was wearing some kind of purple velvet dress that ended just above her knees, striped black & white knee-high stockings, and cherry Doc's with four-inch soles. I thought there might be a bit of running around that day so I'd dressed in cargo shorts, t-shirt and sneakers. Simon was wearing a red Adidas track suit, purchased a decade earlier during a hip-hop phase, while the teens all wore skinny jeans and *Call of Duty* t-shirts - apart from one in a Minecraft singlet who mustn't have got the memo.

After signing waivers and being instructed on how to use the masks and paintball guns, the eight of us were sent into a room with benches to wait for the other team to arrive. We probably should have used that time to discuss strategy but I doubt it would have made a difference. There was a game still in progress when the other team arrived. They entered and waited with us, sitting across the room on facing benches. All eight were dressed head to toe in full military combat gear. Insignia on their shoulders showed a howling wolf silhouetted against a burning moon. They owned their own paintball guns.

"So you guys have played this before?" I asked.
One of them nodded and whispered something to the others.
"We're pretty much fucked, aren't we?" I added.
They all nodded silently.
"Probably should have worn more padding..."

An orange light lit up above the doorway and our teams were ushered into holding areas at opposite ends of a large warehouse. There was scaffolding, barricades and graffitied car bodies between us. A buzzer sounded, the lights dimmed, and the holding area door opened. With no game plan, we ran for cover behind barricades and waited. It was very quiet. I could hear myself and others breathing heavily. Had the other team even entered yet? I leant towards Simon to ask and saw his head snap violently back, engulfed in green splatter from at least five paintballs striking his mask. He landed on his back, threw his gun away and crawled quickly towards the exit. Another two or three paintballs hit him in the legs and back on his way out. I heard shots and several muffled thuds nearby - the teens sprinted towards the exit a few seconds later without their weapons.

Cathy, crouched a yard from me behind the same barricade, looked over at me and raised her sausage claw as if to ask, "What do we do?"

"Cover me," I yelled, hoping she would think I had a plan other than making it to the exit without being hit. Credit where credit's due; she nodded, let out a guttural scream and stood up firing. A paintball immediately hit her in the neck, just under her mask, another ten or so struck her mask and chest. She went down with a thud, flailing and screaming and firing blindly. I took at least five of her shots to my torso, two to my legs and one to my groin.

The paintballs hurt a lot more than I thought they would, I'd expected a thud of sorts, maybe a light slap. It felt like being struck with a hammer and I screamed for her to stop. Another round hit me directly in the right nipple. I fired back. She was a large target and I hit her ten, twenty, thirty times. I must have advanced at some point because by the time I ran out of paintballs, I had a knee on her chest. The lights came up and Simon ran towards us. He pushed me off Cathy and lifted her mask. She was sobbing hysterically, eyes wide and mouth open. There was a fair amount of spittle and a snot bubble made it to the size of a golf ball before popping.

"Did we win?" I asked.

Blink 182

I know a guy named Roger who got his bottom lip pierced because my friend Bill told him he looked like the lead singer of Blink 182. When Roger showed us afterwards, Bill said, "Oh, I meant the lead singer of Phish."

Roger's lip became infected and, despite a course of antibiotics, turned into what looked like mango puree. Eventually he had to have a chunk removed and the two sections of bottom lip sewn together. The reduced width pulled the top lips in at the sides and now he permanently looks like he is about to say something.

"And, if you look at the next slide, you'll see we have... yes Roger?"
"What? I didn't say anything."
"Sorry, I thought you were about t... yes Roger?"

Thanksgiving

The only thing edible at Holly's parent's Thanksgiving dinners are the Dry Balls - bits of bread dipped in milk, rolled into a ball, and baked. Which may sound dreadful, but they come with a cold white sauce made of milk and flour that helps you swallow them. After everyone finishes eating, we sit in the living room watching The Weather Channel for an hour or two in silence. Occasionally someone will comment on how good the Dry Balls were but conversation is kept to a minimum as Holly's father Tom, who is going deaf, makes a big production of turning the television sound down every time someone speaks then turning it back up to its highest setting when they've finished.

"The Dry Balls were good this year, Tom"
"What?"
"The Dry Balls."
"Hang on," 📶 "What?"
"I was just saying the Dry Balls were particularly good this year. Best Dry Balls I've ever had in fact."
"What about the Dry Balls?"
"They were good."
"Marie, what did he say?"
"He said the Dry Balls were good."
"Oh." 📶

Ace Frehley

When I was about ten, my best friend Michael and I discovered a pond at the end of a gravel road. I suppose it belonged to a farmer or something. We'd often ride to the pond after school and on weekends to play, as the town we lived in only had one television station. Once, as we approached the pond, we heard voices. Hiding our bikes in the brush, we crept forward to look over an embankment and discovered a teenage couple kissing below us. The boy had his hand down the front of the girl's jeans and she was giggling and telling him to stop. Suddenly, the boy leapt up and rushed to the edge of the pond. He knelt down, reached out into the water, and lifted out a turtle.

"Check this out," he said, holding the turtle up to show the girl, "I caught a turtle."
"What are you going to do with it?" asked the girl.
"Smash its shell," the boy replied. He put the turtle on the ground, looked around until he found a decent sized rock, and raised it above his head.

A fist-sized rock hit the boy in the side of his head, throwing him sideways into the water. The girl screamed. I looked around, and up, at Michael. He was on his feet, a second rock ready, with a look of pure anger on his face.

The boy sat up in the water, lifted his hand to his head unsteadily, and pulled it away covered in blood. Michael leapt over the embankment, grabbed the turtle, and yelled, "Run!" as he legged it past the boy and girl into the woods. It was pretty much the second bravest thing I've ever seen anyone do.

Michael named the turtle Ace Frehley and kept him in his above ground swimming pool for a few days until his mother made him take it back to the pond. It was probably for the best as their pool was over-chlorinated and Ace Frehley just sat on a boogie board looking sad. Every time we went to the pond after that and saw a turtle, Michael declared, "That's Ace Frehley, I can tell by the shell."

He said it about a flat rock once though so there's no way of knowing if he was ever right. One time however, he waved to a turtle sitting on a partly submerged tree branch and called out, "Hello, Ace Frehley," and, I kid you not, the turtle lifted its front foot for a few seconds as if waving back. Maybe it *was* Ace Frehley. Maybe turtles just lift their legs sometimes.

Part of the Family

I bought part of a racehorse once. One-third of a whole one, not just a leg or anything. I'd worked at a horse-riding school many years before and stayed friends with the owner's son, Michael, who convinced me that it would be a good investment. It was almost three-thousand dollars but, for the cost of the buy-in and a third of *Run Harder*'s upkeep costs, I'd be rewarded with a third of the winnings.

There weren't any winnings. Run Harder was a good looking horse - almost 17 hands with a dark bay coat and white blaze - but she was basically a turd in a ribbon. Her ratio of visits to the vet versus visits to the racetrack was thirty-six to two. Of the two races she ran in, she came last in the first and fell in the second. She hadn't even tripped on anything, it was if she'd been running and then decided, "Fuck this, I'm going to see how far I can slide." Her legs locked up like one of those fainting goats you see in Youtube videos and she slid on her side for about twenty feet. I was actually thankful when she was put down, which I realise is a dreadful thing to say but I was in ten-thousand and getting deeper when she broke her leg. It cost twelve-hundred dollars to have her put down - another three-hundred to have the body disposed of. I could have backed over her with a car a few times for free and rolled her down a creek.

I know an elderly couple, Jack and Carol, who have spent over twenty-thousand in vet bills on their poodle. The poor thing is about six-hundred in human years, blind and deaf, and both its rear legs have been amputated due to cancer. They bought it one of those little harnesses with wheels on the back so it could get around but it developed arthritis in its front legs so it just stays in one spot now.

I'm honestly not sure what the point of keeping the poodle alive any further is. It's fed twice a day and carried outside to defecate but apart from that, it just lies on the couch struggling to breathe and smelling like weird warm cheese. Possibly from vomiting every five minutes from the bucket of painkillers it's on every day.

"What's the funnel for?"
"Time for her pills."
"You don't think, you know, it might be time?"
"No, plenty of life left in the old gal yet."
"Where?"
"She'll be right as rain after her operation next week."
"Another operation? How many does that make?"
"Eighty-two."
"What's this one for?"
"The cancer moved to her front legs. She's having them removed. And her tongue."
"Just let the poor fucking thing die, Jack."
"No."

I'm fairly certain Jack and Carol are going to end up with nothing but the poodle's head on some kind of apparatus to keep the brain functioning. They'll argue that she's 'part of the family' and post pictures of the head wearing a Santa hat on their joint Facebook page at Christmastime. People will comment, "OMG!! So cute!!!!!!!!!!" and, "She's looking so well!" and Jack and Carol will respond with, "Yes, two more operations to remove her jaw and nose and she'll be fit as a fiddle. We've set up a Gofundme page to cover some of the veterinary costs as we're $500,000 in arrears and living in our car by a river."

I get that people love their pets but there has to be a point where people say enough is enough. I'm pretty much ready to have our dogs put down when their toenails need clipping. Or when Holly orders $300 worth of crap from Chewy.com.

"Do they actually need any more dog toys, Holly?"
"Yes."
"There's a huge pile of them in the corner and at least fifty under the couch."
"They get bored of their old toys. Look! This one's an octopus!"
"The dogs don't know what an octopus is. It's shaped like an octopus to please the owner, not the pet. To them, it's just a ball with eight pieces of rope attached. Like all their other balls with rope attached."
"Bullshit. They've been to the beach. Look! This one's a dinosaur. Rawr!"

Holly once ordered steps for the dogs. Carpeted steps. So the dogs could walk up carpeted steps to get onto our bed. The bed the dogs aren't allowed on. She went with the green carpet colour option because, "It looks like grass, the dogs will think they're running up a hill."

I threw the steps out while Holly was at work because A. Our dogs are huge - both can just step onto the bed, and B. They looked like one of those sets photographers sit children on to take studio photos. Usually there'd be a sunny day backdrop, maybe with a field, but in this case it was a bed.

"You don't think it looks a bit molesty?"
"What?"
"All it's missing is a camera on a tripod and a frightened child undressing."
"You hate the dogs, don't you?"
"Yes."

When Holly arrived home and discovered I'd thrown the steps out, she stated, "Well that was a waste of three-hundred and forty dollars."

Blisters

I've only ever been fishing twice - once with Greg Norman and a guy who rollerskated in Xanadu, and once with my friend Geoffrey. Geoffrey borrowed his father's small dinghy and fishing gear one day and we launched, mid morning, in a small bay protected from large waves by outer reefs. We rowed around a bit for no particular reason and then threw the anchor over. The first few minutes of fishing were okay. It became a bit boring after that.

"I should have bought Scrabble." I said to Geoffrey.
"Fishing is about relaxing," he told me, "Take your top off and get a tan."
"I might just do that actually. It's very sunny and nobody is going to see me out here."
We both took our tops off and made ourselves comfortable at opposite ends of the dinghy.
"I should have brought a hat," I commented.
"What hat? I've never seen you wearing a hat."
"No, I'm not big on hats. I should buy one though. For fishing on sunny days. Maybe a Fedora."
"A sombrero would work a lot better."
"Would you wear a sombrero?"
"Yes."
"No you wouldn't. I should have brought a hat and Scrabble."

Geoffrey dug around in a pocket of his cargo shorts, "I brought a joint."

I'm not sure if it was the marijuana or a combination of the marijuana, sun, and how boring fishing is, but we both fell asleep. Geoffrey woke me five hours later by yelling. I bolted upright and also yelled. From our knees down and waist up, we were both scarlet red. Yellow blisters had formed and some popped, leaking clear fluid, as I watched. We sat at each end of the dinghy sobbing with our limbs outstretched.

With a lot of complaining, we managed to pull the anchor up and took an oar each. It was excruciating to bend so we used the oars as paddles. Geoffrey dropped his and we had to let it go so we took it in turns with one. We didn't cover much distance and we needn't have bothered as a larger fishing boat came past and rescued us a few hours later. They radioed ahead to have an ambulance waiting.

Due to a communication error about picking up two sunburnt and dehydrated fishermen, there was also a couple of reporters with cameras from the local news station waiting. We made the news that night; the video clip showed Geoffrey and I being loaded into an ambulance on stretchers. A reporter asked Geoffrey how long we had been adrift and Geoffrey answered, "All day."

Cocksucker

My parents were never really big on discipline. I wasn't smacked or beaten, but I did have to listen to the "We're not angry, we're just disappointed" speech a lot. The only physical punishment I remember receiving was having my mouth washed out with soap. I was seven. My father switched channels to the news while I was watching *The Goodies* and, having heard a term that day at school and assuming it was a generic one like ragamuffin or boofhead, I called him a cocksucker.

Dragged down the hallway and into the bathroom, what I recall of the punishment wasn't the taste of soap, but the fact that the only bar available was a mushy blob stuck to the tiled floor of the shower. As I spat the soap, and a toenail, into the sink afterwards, I remember thinking, 'Nobody in our family has short, thick, curly hair, whose hair is this?'

I mentioned the the soap incident to my father a few years back and he said, "Bullshit. It was Brut-33 soap-on-a-rope. It was hanging on the tap. That's what the rope is for you fucking liar."

Dancing

I can't dance. I've tried on several occasions and fully accept the fact that I look like a marionette walking up stairs while holding two lit candles. People have declared, "Of course you can dance, David, you're just being self-conscious, stop worrying about what anyone else thinks and simply move your body to the beat." But then if I do, they say, "Okay, perhaps you should stop. Are all of your other motor-skills intact? Can you drive a car with a manual gearbox?"

I wish I could dance. I'd dance all the time. I'd be that fun partner that drags Holly onto the dance floor and cuts loose in a fashion nobody would ever describe as pushing a wheelbarrow through mud or inflating an air mattress with a foot pump while playing Whac-A-Mole. People would say, "Gosh, David, you're an amazing dancer. Have you considered dancing professionally?" and I'd reply, "No, I only dance for the love of it. But thank you."

Pineapple

The whole anti-pineapple bias gets a bit old and I'm pretty sure people just pretend to dislike pineapple on pizza because it's a thing and people like to be a part of things.

"Oh, you can't stand pineapple on pizza? No problem, I'll put caterpillars on yours instead."
"Why would I want caterpillars on my pizza?"
"It's a choice between caterpillars or pineapple I'm afraid."
"I'll have pineapple then."
"Yes, I thought as much."
"Well the alternative was a bit extreme."
"Fine. Pineapple or meat?"
"What kind of meat?"
"Caterpillar."

St. Judes

I donate monthly to St. Jude's Children's Hospital. Not because I want to, but because I donated once after seeing their television commercial and then someone rang me to tell me that if I didn't make monthly payments, they'd have to send all the kids home to die. I'm not sure why I fell for the commerical; I've worked in advertising and know exactly how it all works.

"Can someone swap this child for a more attractive one please? Preferably one that's able to smile on cue despite the pain. Is that really too much to ask?"
"How about this one?"
"No, she's not bald enough. And she's Mexican. Nobody in America wants to see Mexican kids getting free cancer treatment. We might stick a black kid in somewhere for legal reasons, but only one and it has to be from a talent agency. We can shave its head if we need to, it's in their contract."
"What about this one? He's white, completely bald, and the pain from eighteen bone marrow transplants has contorted his face into a permanent smile."
"Fine, he'll do. Just stick a few more tubes up his nose and give him a colouring book. I don't want to be here all day, it's fucking depressing."

Bed Bath & Beyond

While shopping in Bed Bath & Beyond with Holly recently, I caught my reflection in the X10 side of a bathroom magnifying mirror and have decided I'm never standing within twenty feet of anyone ever again.

Before that moment, I believed I looked 'somewhere in my early forties' but the magnified mirror informed me I could pass for Walter Matthau's dad. It also let me know that there was a thick black hair, approximately a centimetre long, growing out of one of the manhole sized pores in my nose.

"Holly, there's a thick black hair growing out of my nose."
"Yes, it's hard to miss."
"What? How long has it been there?"
"I don't know, six months."
"And you didn't think to mention it?"
"I figured you'd seen it."
"And what, I decided to keep it? To see how long it would get? Why would I do that?"
"Who knows why you do half the things you do."

Baby Carrot

I saw a movie once called *Lock, Stock and Two Smoking Barrels* in which one of the guys had an idea to make money by placing an ad in specialist magazines for a super orgasm inducing vibrator for thirty dollars - cheques made payable to BTD Ltd. After the money is collected, a reply is sent saying there has been a problem with stock and they receive a refund cheque from Butt Tickler Dildos Ltd. Less than half the people will cash that cheque with their bank.

I was watching the movie with my friend Mark and he said, "I would definitely cash the cheque."
"Does that mean you would buy a super orgasm inducing vibrator from a magazine?" I asked.
"No," he replied, "I'd buy an electric toothbrush and take the bristle bit off and put a baby carrot on it instead."

Which shows he'd thought about this previously. I stopped hanging around Mark a few years later when he went on a health kick, gave up drugs, and, after discovering yoga, felt it important to discuss yoga at every opportunity. It didn't matter what the conversation was about, yoga was the answer. I once asked him his opinion regarding a Pantone colour swatch and although the answer wasn't yoga, I could tell he was thinking about yoga at the time.

Number Plate People

"We should go to Tasmania," Geoffrey stated.

He turned his laptop towards me to present a photo of a woman posing on a trail in a rainforest. Geoffrey and I had been friends since working together at a printing firm years before. He was currently employed as a tech specialist for a local school and I was in my fourth and final year of studies. It was April, 1996.

"Why," I asked, "would I want to go to Tasmania?"
"To have a look," he replied, "It's supposed to be nice. It's the Apple Isle."

Tasmania is at the bottom of Australia, to the right, separated from the mainland by ocean. It's shaped kind of like an apple and its main export to the mainland is apples. It gets left off a lot of maps, which Tasmanians carry on about but nobody listens.

"I've seen apples," I told him. "If I could afford a holiday, I would go somewhere where they have things I haven't seen."
"It wouldn't cost much," Geoffrey argued, "we could drive there."
"You mean I could drive there."

Geoffrey didn't own a car and caught the bus most places.

"They have a boat that ferries cars across. It costs... fifty-five dollars per vehicle under two tons. That's a bargain. How much does your car weigh?"
"Why would I know how much my car weighs?"
"Right. Hang on," he typed something into Alta Vista and waited patiently.

This was before Google was a thing. Or wi-fi. We had to plug a box into the telephone, run a cable to the computer, edit scripts so they would work with the box, try several different ppp settings, unplug the cables, plug them back in...

"We've got two flashing green lights on the modem now, what did you do?"
"I changed 255.255.182.4 to 255.255.182.5, hang on, I'll try 255.255.182.6"
"Three flashing green lights!"
"What do the flashing lights mean?"
"I'm not sure but three has to be better than two. Try changing it to 255.255.182.7... no, they're all off now."

"Ok," said Geoffrey, "It says here that a Fiat 124 Coupé weighs 2,205 pounds. That's around a ton. Even with our bags it will be well under the weight limit."

I'd traded up from a yellow 73' Honda hatchback after it broke in half while on the hoist at Ultra Tune getting the brake pads replaced. Apparently the chassis was completed rusted out and the front and back were only held together by the exhaust pipe. The green 75' Fiat seemed like an upgrade at the time but it was nowhere near as reliable. Due to something amiss with the electrical wiring, it occasionally started itself, and there was always a coolant puddle in the driveway large enough that it needed to be leapt over.

"I doubt the Fiat would make it that far," I said, "it's only running on three cylinders and the radiator is shot."
"I'll pay for your car to be fixed and we can go halves in fuel. Motels are cheap if you're not fussy about sleeping arrangements. If we go for a week the entire holiday will only cost a few hundred dollars. It will be a road trip."
"You'll pay to have my car fixed?"
"Yes."
"I don't actually have any assignments due."
"Excellent."

The drive from Adelaide to Melbourne, where we had to catch the ferry, took just over fourteen hours. It's an eight hour drive but we had to keep stopping to top up the radiator. Geoffrey's idea of paying to have the car fixed had consisted of purchasing a bottle of Wynn's Radiator Stop Leak and a new set of wiper blades.

"If we're going to be touring the 'apple isle' by car, we want a clean windshield to look out of. You don't have to pay me back for those. They were only four dollars."

As we missed the ferry by five hours and had to rebook for the next day, we spent the night in the ferry parking lot.

When the movie *The Mask* first came out, someone told Geoffrey that he did an excellent impression of the bit where Jim Carey says, "Smokin!" Since then, he was convinced that his Fred Flintstone, Crocodile Dundee and John Cleese impressions were nothing short of a gift for others to experience. It was a very long night.

"This parrot is dead! He's an ex parrot. Bereft of life."
"Yes, I've seen it, Geoffrey."
"No, you're meant to say, 'He's just resting.'"
"Can't we play I-spy instead?"
"Fine. I'll go first. I spy with my little eye, something beginning with an F."
"Well it's certainly not a ferry."
"No, but it's got the word ferry in it."
"What?"
"Yes, it's got three words."
"That's a sentence."
"No, it's a name. Of a place."
"Fuck that then, I'm not playing anymore. What was it?"
"Ferry Booking Office."
"I'm really tempted to drive the car off the edge of the dock right now and drown us both. What's the time?"
"11.15, so..." he counted off fingers, "eighteen hours and fifteen minutes until we get to board. You know what we should do?"

"What?"

"Hum parts of a song and the other person has to guess what the song is."

"I'm going to go to sleep."

"Oh no, don't do that. Then I'll be awake by myself and there's nothing to do. Come on, I'll start. Hmmm hmmm, hmm, hmmm hmmm hmm, hmm."

"*Bohemian Rhapsody?*"

"No. It didn't sound anything like *Bohemian Rhapsody*, you must be tone deaf. Here, I'll do it again. Hmm hmm, hmmm, hmm hmm hmm."

"That sounded completely different from the first time."

"That's because I did a different bit. That was the chorus. Do you want me to hum it again?"

"No, I give it up. What was it?"

"*Don't You Want Me* by The Human League."

"What time is it now?"

"11.18."

At 4.30pm the next day, we were first in line to drive aboard. The ship was essentially a floating parking deck. Due to the booking change, the only tickets available were 'Ocean Recliner' which meant sitting in a chair overnight, with no shower facilities, after spending thirty-six hours in the car. A few chairs down from us, a couple had a child with a toothache and a set of healthy lungs but we managed to get a few minutes of sleep regardless. We drove off the ship into Devonport at 6.00 the next morning leaving a large puddle behind.

Devonport looked a lot like Adelaide and I've never been that impressed with Adelaide. We filled the radiator and headed south. Our original five-day plan was to tour the island in a clockwise route with overnight stays in Launceston, Hobart, Queenstown and Burnie before arriving back in Devonport for departure. With only four days, we decided to bypass Launceston and head straight to Hobart.

"We should stop and buy apples," declared Geoffrey. We were driving through farming land and every few miles, kiosks selling apples were set up at the front of properties.
"Why?" I asked.
"We're in the Apple Isle. We have to buy apples. Tasmania is famous for them. People will ask us about the apples when we get back and what are you going to tell them? That we didn't try any? That's just ridiculous."
"I'm fairly certain they're the same apples we buy in Adelaide. All our apples come from here."
"Yes, but these ones haven't been in a truck or boat. Besides, we need snacks for the road trip. Pull over at this one."

Geoffrey purchased two large bags from the vendor, a woman with no teeth, who told us we were going in the wrong direction. We headed back the way we had come looking for the turnoff.

"Do you want one?" Geoffrey offered the bag to me.
"No thanks."

"You're not even going to try one?"

"I kind of like the green ones better. They're more crisp."

"These are pretty crisp," Geoffrey replied, "Listen..." he took a large bite.

"I stand corrected. That did indeed sound crisp."

"Do you want one then?"

"No thanks."

"Fine. All the more apples for me. I'm fairly sure that was the turnoff by the way."

"What?"

"You missed the turnoff."

"Well why didn't you tell me it was coming up?"

"You're the one driving."

"Yes, and you're navigator," I countered, "You have the map."

During our trip across on the ferry, we'd taken time out from our designated chairs to eat at the cafeteria. It was slim pickings, pre-wrapped sandwiches and the like, and we had to line up with trays like they make you do at IKEA. Our tray liners, an A3 piece of paper, featured an outline of Tasmania, with landmarks, for kids to colour in with a supplied small box of crayons. The crayons, four per box, were only slightly thicker than a piece of wire and one of them was white. They kept snapping and were constructed from a material not unlike crayon, but not similar enough to leave much of a mark on paper. Our proposed route was marked in purple crayon with tourist locations we intended to visit coloured in green. Geoffrey had also shaded the shoreline in with blue.

"The map doesn't show the turnoff. It just has a picture of a turtle. I'm going by what the old lady told me. She said to turn left at the big rock shaped like a boot. That road will take us to a main road that goes all the way to Hobart."
"Was there a rock shaped like a boot?"
"Kind of."
"Right. I'll keep going for a bit then and if we don't see a rock that is definitely shaped like a boot, we'll head back."
"No, it was definitely boot shaped."

I turned the car around and drove back. The rock wasn't shaped anything like a boot.

"Maybe you misunderstood because of her thick Tasmanian accent and lack of teeth."
"No," Geoffrey replied, "She definitely said boot. Maybe it depends on which angle you look at it from."
"It's round. Whatever angle you look at it from, it's going to be round. Perhaps you should have asked her what kind of boot; a boot shaped one or the round kind."
"It's not perfectly round, it has a bit that sticks up at the back. I can definitely see a kind of boot shape."

We took the turnoff. It led to a farmhouse so we reversed back down their driveway and continued on along the highway until we found the correct landmark. It *was* actually shaped like a boot. Someone had spray-painted black laces on it. Someone else had spray-painted the words *Ken Matthews is a wanker* in white.

"Oh yes," said Geoffrey, "I saw that when we drove past earlier."
"You knew where the boot was?"
"It didn't register that it was boot-shaped at the time. I was too busy wondering who Ken Matthews is and if he has seen that rock. He would have been pretty cross."

During the five hour drive to Hobart, Geoffrey made me play a game that he invented called *Number Plate People*. As cars passed us, we had to record the letters and numerals from their number plate and use each letter as the first letters of someone's name. GZA-426 for example, became Glen, Zoe, Alice. The numbers indicated the probability of the person driving the car being called either Glen, Zoe or Alice. In this case, a 4 in 26 chance. It was far more excruciating than I am making it sound.

"Losing that day has really mucked up our schedule," Geoffrey complained as he marked our new route on the map. He'd tried colouring over the old route with the white crayon but it hadn't worked. He held it up. "Ignore everything in purple. Everything green is where we are going now. Except the green whale."
"Right, well you're the navigator. We've already established your skills in that area."
"Okay, because we lost a day, and it's now nearly noon on Sunday, we should turn left up here. That will take us to Port Arthur."
"What's at Port Arthur?"

"Its the ruins of an old prison."

"Oh good. I thought we were going straight to Hobart but visiting prison ruins sounds much better than food and a shower."

"We can eat at Port Arthur, "Geoffrey replied, "They have a cafe. If we go to Hobart first, we won't have time to get to the prison before it closes and I will have to colour over it with purple. I know how long it takes you to shower."

When I was growing up, my father had very strict water usage rules. If using the sink, under no circumstances were we to use the hot tap. If using the shower, we were not to exceed three minutes. He would set a timer and if the water was still on when the buzzer went off, he'd barge into the bathroom yelling and turn it off. He was a bit of a dick. As the shower took a few minutes to warm up, we had to lather ourselves with soap and shampoo outside the stream and use the remaining sixty seconds to wash it off. After my father left us, everyone took as long as they fucking wanted in the shower. Since then, my showers have extended to two, sometimes three, hours. I usually turn on the shower and make a coffee while waiting for it to get nice and steamy. Then I get in and have my coffee with a cigarette. After enjoying the water for a while, I shave, brush my teeth, shampoo my hair and wash. In that order but the time between each varies. Then I enjoy the water for a while. Sometimes I try to drown a bug or see how much water I can hold with my arms crossed or hold my arms down with my fingers splayed to make the water run off the tips. My current bathroom has a television and coffee machine in it. I tried putting a beanbag in the shower but, after a few months, the stitching rotted away and it burst so now I use a camping chair.

The Port Arthur Historical Site was an hour out of our way. Geoffrey suggested we continue our game of Number Plate People and I threatened to swerve into oncoming traffic.

"Let's play *Science Fiction Movies* then. I'll say a science fiction movie and whatever letter it ends with, you have to name a science fiction movie that starts with that letter."
"Righto," I agreed, "*Star Wars.*"
"No, I go first."
"Okay."
"*Star Wars.*"
"Really Geoffrey? Fine. *Star Wars, The Empire Strikes Back.*"
"No, you can't use *Star Wars* movies twice in a row."
"Are you just saying that because you can't think of a science fiction film that starts with K?" I asked.
"No."
"Fine, *Spaceballs* then."
"That's really more of a comedy than science fiction, but I'll let you have it. *Star Wars, The Empire Strikes Back.*"
"Right, I'm not playing anymore."
"Oh come on."
"No. I wouldn't have thought it possible ten minutes ago, but you actually managed to come up with a game more painful than *Number Plate People.*"

"Let's play *Animals* then."

"Do you name an animal and I use the last letter to name another animal?"

"No," I make an animal sound and you have to guess what it is. I'll go first. Araack!"

"That just sounded like someone yelling the name Eric. Is it Eric's mother?"

"No, it's Araack!, not Eric. I'll give you a clue, it's brown."

"That's not much of a clue. Most animals are brown."

"Yes, but only one of them says Araack!"

"Is it a camel?"

"No."

I give up then. What was it?

"Oh don't give up yet," Geoffrey moaned, "I'll give you one more clue. It has long eyelashes."

"That's all I get to go on? It's brown, has long eyelashes, and yells Eric?"

"Araack!"

"Right, well I don't give a fuck what it is, it sounds dreadful."

"It was a seal."

"It didn't sound anything like a seal. Seals bark."

"No, that's dogs. Because you didn't get it, I get to go again. Braaad!"

We arrived and drove through a toll booth and into the parking lot just after 1pm. It was a nice day, warm with blue skies and a light breeze. There were quite a few tourists. Geoffrey consulted the brochure we'dd been given.

"What do you want to look at first?"
"Where's the cafe?" I asked.
Geoffrey consulted the brochure again. It had a little map on the back. He pointed to a building.
"That's the gift shop and cafe," he said, "but we should look at the ruins first. I'm not really all that hungry."
"Really? You only ate two bags of apples. You don't want a barrel of plums or a bucket of apricots to go with them? I'm going to get something to eat."

We made our way up the steps of the building and entered through the gift shop. I bought a black and white striped t-shirt with 'Inmate of Port Arthur Prison' written on it. Geoffrey bought a coffee mug and a fridge magnet.

The cafe had the IKEA tray system so we grabbed a tray each and made our way down the line. I had my eye on a cherry danish but the man in front of us took it.

"Good choice," I said, "I was going to get that."
The man turned and frowned. He had blonde wavy hair, parted in the middle, and was carrying a big bag.
"You can have it if you like. It's burnt on the edges. I don't like them when they're overcooked."
He offered the danish to me.
"No, no. You enjoy your cherry danish. I'm sure it will be delicious despite the burnt edges."
"I don't mind."
"I'll have it then," said Geoffrey. He took the danish.

The man with the blonde wavy hair and I both selected a slice of carrot cake instead.

"Snap." I said.

"What?"

"Snap. You know, the card game."

"No. Is it like Uno?"

"Not really."

"It's more like Go Fish," Geoffrey interjected helpfully.

"No, it's not," I told the man with blonde wavy hair, "Don't listen to him. He's insane."

"It's for the same age group," Geoffrey argued.

"Right, so by that argument, Slip'n'Slide is also similar to Snap."

"I've never played Slip Inside so I wouldn't know," said Geoffrey, "Is it like Go Fish?"

"Are you serious? Slip'n'Slide. The long piece of yellow plastic that you put on your lawn, spray water on, and kids slide down."

"Oh, you mean the Splash'n'Ride'?

"What the fuck? Who calls it the Splash'n'Ride?

"That's what the one we had was called."

"You must have had a cheap Chinese knockoff then, the real one is called Slip'n'Slide. Where'd you get it?"

"I'm not sure. Maybe Target. Can you pass me one of those Splades please?"

Further up the line, I added a cheese sandwich and a bag of chips to my tray. Geoffrey selected a banana to "mix things up a bit." I have no idea what the man with the blonde wavy hair added because Geoffrey and I were busy arguing whether the plastic spoons with a built-in fork were called splades or sporks. We paid for our meal and made our way outside to eat on the balcony. Wasps hovered near an open bin by the door so I carried on a bit and we sat at a table towards the back. I'm not a fan of wasps.

Once when I was young, my family drove up the coast to stay at a beachside town called Kalbari during summer break. We rented a cabin at the Kalbarri Caravan Park. There was a small shack on the beach that rented snorkelling equipment so my sister and I hurriedly searched through bags for our swimming outfits while my father walked around with his hands on his hips, nodding and commenting on what an excellent choice in accommodation he had made.

"Look, ceiling fans. Very nice. The ceiling appears to be bowing here though, and there's a stain in the middle that looks wet."

He reached up on tippy toes and poked the wet spot with his finger. His finger went straight through, opening a hole about an inch in diameter. Wasps poured out of the hole. Thousands of them. The room looked like yellow and black static. Everyone was stung multiple times but my father took the brunt of the attack. After he was released from hospital, my mother had to drive the car home because my father couldn't open his eyes due to the swelling. It was the third worst holiday I have ever been on.

The man with the blonde wavy hair sat a few tables down from us. He smiled and raised his spork with a bit of carrot cake on it as way of a salute.

"They're not European wasps so you don't have to worry," he said.

"Sorry?"

"Those are just normal wasps. There's a lot of wasps about today but I haven't seen any European wasps."

"What's the difference?" Geoffrey asked, seemingly quite interested, "Is there a noticeable size or colour variation?"

The man with the blonde wavy hair seemed pleased at this engagement.

"They're the same colour but European wasps are smaller than normal wasps. They look more like bees. A man came to our house and hung European wasp traps on the trees in our backyard because our neighbour's had a nest of them in their shed. I looked in one and it was full of dead European wasps. We've got lots of European wasps in Tasmania but those," he indicated towards the bin, "are just Yellow Paper Wasps. They won't kill you."

"Well that's good to hear," said Geoffrey, 'You certainly know a lot about wasps."

"That's because I'm a wasp scientist," said the man with the blonde curly hair, "that's my job."

"Really?" I asked, "Why didn't you put the traps on the trees yourself then?"

Geoffrey kicked my leg under the table.

"It's a valid question," I continued, "Had you run out of your own wasp traps? As a wasp scientist, it might be assumed that you'd have an abundant supply."

"So," said Geoffrey, attempting to change the subject, "you live around here then? That must be nice."

"Apart from all the wasps of course," I added, "You'll probably be on top of that though once you get some more traps."

Geoffrey kicked me again.

The man with the blonde curly hair nodded, "Are you from the mainland?"

"Yes," Geoffrey answered, finishing the last bite of his banana, "Adelaide. It's a shithole."

Adelaide isn't a shithole. It has some nice bits. It's the people that live in Adelaide that ruin it. Seen as a kind of joke by the rest of Australia, Adelaidians spend a lot of their time trying to convince themselves, and other Adelaidians, that they are not a joke and are actually fairly damn awesome. This means dressing in the latest European fashions, even just to visit the supermarket, and pretending they spend a lot of time in Melbourne and Sydney. Adelaide is more like a large village than a city. A village where the idiots outnumber normal townsfolk a hundred to one and they all wear G-Star and Diesel. The tourism slogan for Adelaide is, *It's Heaps Good*. I wish I was making this up.

We left our trays on a counter near the bins, dodged a few wasps, and wandered down a grassy hill towards the ruins. Behind us, the man with the blonde wavy hair finished his meal and carried his big bag back inside the cafe.

"I've never met a wasp scientist before," I said to Geoffrey, "I certainly learnt a lot."

"He seemed harmless enough," Geoffrey replied, "You have to expect Tasmanians to be a little odd. They don't have much to do apart from growing apples so they probably get a bit bored and make up stories to sound more interesting. Stand on top of that rock and I'll take a photo."

"I'll stand next to it. People are watching."

"Just stand on it." he replied, "How is standing *next* to a rock even remotely interesting? We should make it our theme."

"Our theme?"

"Yes, the theme of our holiday photos. We stand on a rock in every shot. Oh, no..."

"What?"

"We should have got a photo standing on the rock shaped like a boot."

'Yes," I agreed, "and the round one."

Geoffrey frowned, "No, that would be stupid."

I stood on the rock.

"Okay," Geoffrey queried, "is that what you are going to do? Just stand there? You don't want to pretend you're doing something?"

"Like what?"

"I don't know, pointing at something perhaps."

"No, just take the photo."

"What if you jumped with your arms in the air?"

"Like an action shot?"

"Yes, exactly."

"No, just take the photo."

Inside the café, the man with the blonde wavy hair unzipped his big bag, took out an AR-15 semi-automatic assault rifle, and began shooting patrons and staff.

"Gunshots!" exclaimed Geoffrey, "We're missing a reenactment. I bet a convict has escaped and the prison wardens are chasing him. Let's go watch."
"It's coming from way up the hill." I replied, "We just came from there. They will probably do another one in an hour. Let's just finish looking at rocks and then we can walk back up. It sounds like it's finished anyway."

The man with the blonde wavy hair reloaded the assault rifle and stepped out of the cafe. Tourists heading towards the area hoping to catch part of a reenactment were fired upon.

"No," said Geoffrey, "Listen, it's still going. Quick, take a photo of me standing on the rock and then we'll go watch." Geoffrey climbed onto the rock, looked to his left and held his hand to his forehead.
"Why are you saluting?" I asked.
"I'm not," he replied, "I'm gazing into the distance. Just hurry up and take the shot. We're missing the reenactment."
"Okay," I took the photo, "Now, put your hands on your knees, bend them a little, turn to the side a bit... a bit more, now put your head back and smile."
"You really are a dickhead," Geoffrey said, jumping down.

We were half way back up the hill when an old lady came

tearing down past us. She was a large woman with blue eyeshadow, a tight perm and tighter white slacks. Both her knees had large green grass stains where she had fallen and skidded.

"Run!" she screamed.

We ran. The look on her face as she yelled her warning was all the convincing we needed.

"Is it zombies?" Geoffrey yelled as we passed her.

Many hours later, after police officers took our statements and contact information, we were free to leave. We hadn't been anywhere near the cafe during the shootings so could provide no helpful eyewitness accounts. There was no discussion about driving back to Devonport, I just drove there. Both of us wanted to be home.

"I hope the wasp guy is alright," said Geoffrey.
"I'm sure he's fine," I said, "I didn't see him... you know."
Geoffrey nodded, "They were covered though. It was pretty hard to tell. Some of the sheets were small..."
"Do you want to play *Number Plate People*?" I asked.
"Alright."

Naps

The older I get, the more I understand the whole dozing off thing. I haven't seen the end of a movie in years. Sometimes I'll jolt awake when I hear myself snore, other times I'll do a quick analysis of the pros and cons of napping at that moment. Driving? Probably best to be awake. Watching a Netflix show that Holly has chosen? I don't need to know if the edgy teen lesbian confronts her best friend about the kiss.

Holly blames my naps on never getting a good night's sleep. Apparently due to needing a new mattress and not because Holly performs sleep calisthenics. Forget the whole 'stealing the blanket' thing, Holly rolls up in the blanket like a huge cocoon and uses her legs to push herself around in circles while mumbling, "Come on, we can win this," and "That's not how you swim, you have to use your legs like this."

Holly dragged me mattress shopping recently but there's no way I can test a mattress when the salesman is standing a foot away staring down at me. Go sit behind your little desk and I'll come and get you when I want to know if you have a mattress as comfortable as the $10,000 Hästens Excelsior, but for around the $400 mark. Don't get me started on Sleep Number, I'm not paying that much for a blowup mattress. Coleman sells them for forty bucks.

Helmets

I've never been white-water rafting. Hurtling down a river in an inflatable boat with several other idiots - high-fiving each other the whole time and saying things like 'woo' - is on my reverse bucket-list of stupid things to avoid along with marathons and musical theatre.

"Let's spend the day getting splashed and possibly being thrown onto rocks or into churning water. We get to wear helmets."
"Awesome, what kind of helmets?"
"I'm not sure, I think they're probably like bicycle helmets."
"Sign me up then, that's my favourite type of helmet.

The Meadows

"The name is a bit deceptive, Holly.," I said, "The word meadow implies some kind of field vegetated by grass and other non-woody plants, not trucks, Confederate flags and child molestation."
"There's a field over there."
"That's an airport."
"It's still a field."
"Technically, yes. Not somewhere you'd take the family for a picnic though. I'm going home."
"I promised Ina we'd go to her barbecue, so we're going."
"It's a trailer park. I'm going to be stabbed and you're going to be chained in a shipping container."
"It doesn't look that bad. Look, that trailer has Christmas decorations. With a giant inflatable snowman."
"It's June."
"We're going."
"If you make me, I'm going to sit in the car with the doors locked. I need more emotional preparation for a situation like this. And a different outfit. I'm wearing a t-shirt that says I heart squirrels. I need some kind of thin western shirt with the sleeves cut off. The kind with studs for buttons. And a Pontiac Trans-Am with a gold eagle on the hood."
"You don't like the t-shirt I got you?"
"Yes, I like the t-shirt. Not a big fan of Gildan though."

Unfortunately, Ina saw us and ran out barefooted in bike shorts and a bikini top to guide us to their trailer. I'm not sure where she found a pair of bike shorts that size but whoever sells them has a social responsibility to stop.

We parked next to red Chevy Silverado pickup truck that was lifted so high, the door handles were head height. It had a sticker on the back window that said 'Not My President!' above Obama's face with a red target over it, and a bigger sticker that said Chevrolet. So that people driving behind can tell it's a Chevrolet without having to get too close I suppose.

"What kind of pickup truck is that in front of us?"
"I'm not sure, I'll speed up and check…"
"Just be careful, the roads are icy."
"Oh, wait, it's a Chevrolet. I don't need to drive dangerously because he's got a big sticker on the back window that says Chevrolet. We should get one of those stickers for our Nissan. One that says Nissan obviously, not Chevrolet."
"Yes, we should. You can't put a price on safety."

There were four other guests at the barbecue, not including Ina's boyfriend Luke and their eight children.

One of the guests, a 400-pound man in his fifties named TNT, had one tooth, no shirt, and two crossed sticks of dynamite tattooed on his chest. I asked him what he did and he replied, "Eat pussy."

Two of the guests were Ina's parents. Her father looked like a stick insect wearing a Santa beard and her mother looked like a pudding wearing a wig. They were both deaf so I guess they met at some kind of deaf camp or something. I've got nothing against deaf people but the 'nuhugghnnn' noise gets a bit annoying and there's no point trying to teach me how to say banana with eighty sequential hand movements that look like you're conjuring a water demon because I'm not going to remember it. Just carry a pad and pencil around and either write the word banana or draw one. Also, the jazz fingers instead of clapping thing. Not a huge fan.

I worked with a deaf guy named Neil for a couple of years. He looked like a human/axolotl hybrid and had red hair so there wasn't a lot going for him. We worked in different departments - he was an account rep at Amcor while I worked in the art department - but we often had to drive to attend client meetings together. The trips were excruciating because he drove a manual hatchback and, even at highway speeds, never went above second gear. The engine screamed and the RPM gauge redlined while he sat there oblivious. Sometimes I'd try to alert him to the fact but he'd just smile and nod and say, "Nuhugghnnn." We were late for a meeting one afternoon and, after gunning his vehicle harder than usual, the engine blew up. Cylinders actually punched through the hood and flames came out the air-conditioning vents. Also, if you can't hear people knocking on your office door, perhaps lock it if you're planning on having a lunch wank.

Ina's parents lived in the trailer next door, which was probably quite handy for babysitting and Grits Sunday. Her father invited me over to look at his collection of brown slacks and showed me some kind of special video camera setup on his television for deaf people. I had to sit in a chair and wave at a deaf person in Alaska.

The fourth guest, a blonde woman wearing a hoodie with *Team Jesus* written across it, told me I talked funny and when I explained I was from Australia, she asked if I'd driven to the United States.

"No, there's actually a fair bit of water between the two countries so you'd need some kind of amphibious vehicle."
"What's amphibious mean?"
"Like a frog."
"TNT, this guy says he came to America on a frog."
"No I didn't."
"Have you ever seen a kangaroo?"
"Yes. Thousands."
"Can you ride them?"
"No."
"Have you ever seen an emu?"
"Yes. But it's pronounced 'eem-you' not 'ee-moo'."
"Can you ride eemooyoos?"
"What's your fascination with riding wildlife?"
"I don't have a fascination. Have you ever seen a crocodile?"
"Yes, Queensland beaches are crawling with them. And before you ask, no you can't ride them."

I wouldn't even go knee deep in Queensland; the water there is approximately 20% crocodile. They're salt-water crocodiles so essentially sharks with legs. I read about a woman whose poodle was taken by a crocodile while she was walking it along the beach. They were several feet from the shoreline but the crocodile exploded out of the water and closed the distance in a fraction of a second. It was a relatively small crocodile, only seven or eight feet, but even the babies can do some damage. To her credit, the woman refused to let go of the leash even after the poodle was ripped in half. She ended up with the head and front half so technically she won, but it wasn't much of a prize. I probably would have let the crocodile have it at that stage. Less to clean up.

"Why would anyone want to ride a crocodile? Have you ever seen a dingo?"
"Holly, how long are we staying?"
"A few hours."
"Right. Don't forget we've got that thing later. That thing that we have to go to."
"There's no thing."

There were no seats outside so we all sat inside the trailer on a damp brown velour lounge suite, staring at each other and listening to a Kid Rock CD. Ina had hand painted the phrase *Live, Laugh, Love* in large script above a pot belly stove and we all agreed that it added value to the trailer and that she was like some kind of reincarnation of Gandhi.

There was also no actual barbecue but Luke had slow-cooked a large pot of bear meat stew for two days. We each had to put in five-dollars for it but, because Holly and I are vegetarian and didn't eat, we received a two-dollar discount.

When a bottle of Jim Beam was passed around to swig from - after everyone had finished the beer that Holly and I had brought - we said we were going to get more beer and drove home instead.

Later we learnt that Luke had driven to buy more alcohol, with four children in the back, and rolled his Chevrolet. He was charged with child endangerment, driving under the influence, driving with a suspended license, and driving an unregistered vehicle. He did ninety days in jail and while he was locked up, Ina sold his truck, slept with his brother, and gave TNT a blowjob for twenty-dollars.

Socks

A hint of first light filtered through dusty blinds. Heather yawned and stretched under the warm duvet, reaching for Hank beside her. Hank snorted and rolled over in his sleep. She smiled and snuggled into him, kissed his neck softly and whispered, "I love you, sleepyhead."

She'd gotten a little tipsy the night before, the three boxes of wine and twelve-pack of Keystone Light had gone straight to her head. She didn't blame the alcohol though; she'd wanted it to happen. They'd wrestled playfully on the couch and she'd kissed him during Double Jeopardy. It was a tentative first kiss. The second kiss was long and wet and had a lot of tongue. Heather wore her Wonder Woman costume to bed, Hank wore socks.

She'd have to tell Ian of course. He was in Ohio, delivering airplane armrests for the company he worked for, but he'd be back the next day. As long as he didn't make things weird, he could move into the spare room until he found another place to live.

Throwing back the duvet, Heather climbed out of bed and made her way downstairs to fix breakfast. Hank heard his food bowl being filled and ran downstairs excitedly to join her.

Poetry

I'm not a huge fan of poetry. I'll accept the argument that it's an art form - being an expression of the imagination - but by that broad definition, so are Etch-A-Sketch drawings and Magic Aqua Sand sculptures. I don't think anyone *really* likes poetry, apart from the ones writing it, and they only *really* like their own. People might declare they *really* like poetry but if pressed to name their favourite poem it's generally a struggle.

"Oh, um, probably the one about a tree or *The Road Less Travelled*. It's a classic."
"The 1978 book of psychology and spirituality by M. Scott Peck?"
"No, the poem version. I had to read it in school. It's about a guy who's taking a walk and chooses an overgrown path. It's a metaphor for not worrying about ticks."
"Do you mean *The Road Not Taken*?"
"No, that's a movie about a dad and his son who have to escape from cannibals after the apocalypse. I think Liam Neeson was in it."

Tampa

I flew to Tampa last year and it was the third worst business trip I've ever been on. Firstly, if you have a chance to visit Tampa, choose not to. The city is a shithole and everyone there is insane. Secondly, if you have to go to Tampa, don't go with my coworker Gary. It's like travelling with an angry geriatric five-year-old. He grumbles about everything, from the colour of orange juice to cloud density, and has never heard the term 'pick your battles'.

The flight from D.C. to Tampa is an easy two and a half hours, but in that short period Gary managed to reprimand a female passenger for wearing too much perfume, demanded the cabin temperature be raised because it was 'as cold as a well digger's ass in here', told a male flight attendant not to fuck with him because he knows karate, threatened to sue the airline for bumping his knee with a drink cart, and shouted at a child for crying. I'm not a fan of crying children on airplanes, but I've never had the inclination to yell, "For the love of god, someone smother it!"

I told the flight attendant that Gary had dementia and bought the mother a drink as way of apology. I also used the in-flight wi-fi to change my return seat so I wouldn't be sitting next to Gary.

During the Uber ride to the meeting, Gary loudly stated, "I was expecting a much nicer car. You'd think they'd have to meet some kind of standard."

During the meeting, Gary informed the client that her boardroom chairs were ugly, asked if their windows had ever been cleaned, and took his shoes and socks off.

"Sorry about this, he doesn't get out much."
"Yes I do. I'm very active."
"Belligerence isn't a sport, Gary. Put your shoes back on."
"I can't, my feet are swollen. Look."

The swelling was bad; his feet looked like footballs with toes. Apparently it's called edema. The client gave Gary a Benadryl and a cardboard poster tube to use as a walking cane, but Gary declared himself unable to fly or drive a vehicle, so I had to rent a car and drive nine hundred miles back to D.C. It was like a twelve-hour version of *Driving Miss Daisy* but without the character development and eventual friendship. Just the bits where Miss Daisy complains about the bumps, the climate control settings, and her seat's lack of decent lumbar support. I haven't seen the movie but I assume Miss Daisy and Denzel Washington become friends, despite their differences, and team up to win a race or something. Also, Gary's bladder must be the size of a walnut because we had to stop every half-hour so he could use a restroom. I had to help him in and support him while he urinated, and he pissed on my leg twice.

"Are you sure there are no stations that play Billy Joel?"
"Yes, I checked. Just EDM I'm afraid."
"It's not even real music, it's just microwave button beeps."
"Yes, well, kids these days, huh?"
"I need to use a restroom."
"Again? We stopped ten minutes ago."
"I couldn't go while you were watching me."
"I wasn't watching you, Gary, I was checking your aim. Just use the empty Gatorade bottle I gave you."
"I'm not peeing in a bottle. I'm not an animal."
"Animals don't pee in bottles, Gary. They do, however, sometimes pee on people's legs."
"How many times do you expect me to apologise for the same thing? I said I'd pay for dry cleaning."
"That's not the point. My sock is squelchy and we still have six hundred miles to go."
"You should have packed a spare pair of socks to change into. It's the number one tip for flyers."
"Why would I pack socks for a meeting? It was meant to be a short flight there, short flight back. My itinerary didn't include driving across the country in piss socks."
"My itinerary didn't include being crippled. Sorry to be such a bother. Why don't you just pull over and leave me in a ditch. If I'm lucky, an alligator will eat me."
"It's tempting. Might be a little difficult to explain to Jennifer in HR though. She'd probably make me fill out a form."
"Jennifer is nice."
"Yes, she's very pleasant."
"She's the only one I like at the office."

Hiking

I saw a show on television in which a man wearing a green John Deere cap rolled his dead coworker up in a rug and threw him off a bridge. I came in late to the program so I have no idea how either of them came to be in this situation but I assume they fought over corn or something.

The rug was nice, white with a subtle chequered pattern, and I thought it highly unlikely that someone who wears a John Deere cap would own a contemporary rug like that. People who wear John Deere caps prefer ornate things. A contemporary rug wouldn't go with their green velour couch or the maple and glass cabinet containing ceramic horse figurines. An Oriental or Persian looking rug would make more sense. It wouldn't show the dirt as much. I looked online and found the exact white chequered rug at IKEA for $299 so I ordered it. People who wear John Deere caps don't shop online, or at IKEA, they shop at Grande Home Furnishings & Mattresses.

The man wearing a green John Deere cap was apprehended fairly quickly as the contemporary rug was discovered the next morning with his fingerprints all over the rubber backing. His prints were on file as he had a prior arrest for stealing three rolls of fencing wire from the back of a hardware store. If I ever have to roll a coworker up in a rug and throw him off a bridge, I will remember to roll him up with the carpeted side facing outwards. I'll also take a flashlight with me to check if the creek has any water in it. Also, if I regularly wore a green John Deere cap, I would swap it out for the occasion, perhaps with a beanie, just in case a homeless person living under the bridge later agrees to serve as witness for the prosecution.

I rolled up a rug a few days ago to take it down to the basement. One of our dogs took a huge dump on it and I couldn't get out the stain. I tried moving the furniture around to hide it but wasn't happy with the layout. The rug was pretty heavy. I had to drag it most of the way and needed a nap afterwards. The man wearing a green John Deere cap must have been a lot stronger than me, probably from years of lifting pigs and polishing his tractor, as there's no way I'd manage to lift a rug over a railing if it included a body.

A better solution might be to strap the rug to the roof of your car and park really close to the edge so it can be rolled off - or, keep the rug, especially if it's a nice one, drive the dead coworker out into a forested area, or a park if you live in the city, and sit them against a tree with a compass in one hand and a map of a completely different area in the other. This way it would appear they simply got lost while hiking and did not posess the necessary survival skills to find their way out. You could leave a bag of trail mix with only the bits nobody likes left in their pocket to allay suspicion.

If the coworker is known to enjoy hiking, people will say, "Oh yes, he often went hiking, at least he died doing what he loved," and, if he isn't the type to go hiking, it will explain why he was so bad at it. Before leaving the office and heading out to the forested area, you could use his computer to send the secretary an email stating, "I'm going for a hike."

To prevent this ever happening to me, I tell everyone in the office once a day that I have no interest whatsoever in hiking.

Exercise

I'm not a huge fan of exercise. It seems like a lot of work and rather time consuming. I did participate in a charity run through work once though. It was dreadful.

The charity run was on a work day and I assumed, based on the fitness level of my coworkers, that it would be a brisk walk, interspersed with less-brisk walking, through a park or something. I realized this wasn't the case when we arrived to discover people wearing Fitbits and neon. They were talking about 'times' and doing stretching exercises behind SUVs with bike racks. A large sign over the starting point read:

ANNUAL 5K MUD, SWEAT & CHEERS RUN!

Two of our five member team went home. Joylene from Human Resources and Kevin from Accounts guilt-tripped me into staying. None of us finished. Kevin bowed out when he got a leg-cramp within the first three minutes, Joylene fell hard and lost her glasses in mud on the first obstacle, and I was disqualified for taking a cigarette break behind a log wall.

I'd made it the furthest of our team though so that's not bad. Joylene didn't speak to me for a week but I dismissed her claims of being pushed as fanciful and expecting me to stop to help find her glasses as against the rules.

"Maybe it was just a muscle twinge."
"It wasn't a muscle twinge, I know what a push feels like."
"Well, there's no point speculating about these things."
"I'm not speculating. You pushed me. I made it to the rope platform before you, so you pushed me."
"Muscle twinges can feel like a push. Besides, you wouldn't have made it across anyway. Probably better to go down at the edge where it's shallow than in the middle. Being stuck in the middle would hold up everyone behind you."
"We were last. The only person behind me was you."
"Well there you go. Muscle twinge. Alluding to anything other just makes you come off as a bit of a bad sport. I didn't complete the mud run either."
"No, but you're wearing the t-shirt that says you did."
"I got further than you."

Xanadu

I was quite young when the movie *Xanadu* first came out in theatres, but not too young to be impressed by Olivia Newton John's outfit. I remember being puzzled as to why *all* girls didn't choose to wear flowing white dresses, ribbons in their hair, and roller skates. I wasn't so impressed with Olivia's outfit in *Grease,* although the shiny black pants she wore at the end were ok.

My best friend at the time owned a copy of the album *Physical* that came with a folded poster showing Olivia doing exercises in Spandex leggings and leg warmers. Where the crotch was meant to be, he'd made a hole.

"Why is there a hole in the poster?"
"It came that way."
"But it's all wet."
"Just fold it up and put it back in the cover."

Pickle

I almost killed my coworker Simon once. He'd had a late night and had fallen asleep at his desk, snoring softly with his head back and mouth open, so I stuck a pickle in his mouth. It was a spur of the moment thing and I thought it would funny to see him either bite into the pickle or spit it out in surprise. I wasn't expecting him to gasp and swallow it. It sounded like a hamster being sucked up a vacuum cleaner hose.

Simon's eyes opened, wider than I'd seen them before, and he stared at me in panic while grabbing his throat and doing a weird thing with his head like a chicken pecking corn. I panicked as well and did an on-the-spot dance while shaking my hands in front of me. I'd like to think my panic was due to fearing for Simon's wellbeing, but it was probably the thought of having to explain his death afterwards.

"Yes officer, I've told him several times not to swallow pickles whole but he never listened. I would have attempted to give him the Heimlich maneuver but he had a thing about hugs, I think he was like seventy percent autistic."

It was Rebecca, our project manager, who saved the day. Though short and petite, she lifted Simon out of his chair, swung him around, administering the Heimlich maneuver with one big squeeze. The pickle popped out like a cork and hit the far wall of his office. It was pretty spitty.

It would have been a lot easier for me if Simon had died that day. I had to attend an occupational health and safety course and sign an F26-B formal complaint form stating I had read and understood section 5C of the employee agreement about skylarking. For Secret Santa that year, I gave Simon a jar of pickles but nobody thought it was funny.

Hats off to Rebecca though, she stepped up when I froze. That's difficult for me to admit because I don't like her. She has a huge forehead like Robocop or Ellen Page, and she always has to 'one up' people.

"Sorry I'm late, Rebecca. I didn't get to bed until 2am."
"I didn't get to bed until 8.59am and I still managed to make it to the 9am meeting on time."
"That doesn't seem possible but okay. You do live closer though. I had to drive here in heavy traffic."
"I had to walk. In shoes made out of crushed glass and thumbtacks."
"That's highly unlikely, why would anyone do that?"
"And it was snowing."
"It's summer."
"A bear attacked me. It tore off both my arms."
"I can see you have arms, Rebecca."
"I guess I just have more respect for other people's time."

Rebecca has only lived in the United States a few years longer than I have. She was born in Germany which may explain her unblemished attendance record, crisp outfits, and no-nonsense approach to hairstyles. I'm not a fan of hair buns in general, they look like you're balancing a coconut on your head, but surely someone at some point has suggested bangs to her. I don't wish to harp on about the size of her forehead, but, honestly, you could land a helicopter on it. It's also a well-established fact that Germans have no sense of humour.

"Hans, I have a very funny joke for you."
"Proceed, Fritz."
"There is something on your foot."
"There is? I see nothing."
"It is your shoe."
"That is a very clever joke. You could be a professional comedian. Do you have another?"
"Yes. How many Dutch people does it take to screw in a lightbulb?"
"It is not a complicated task so my guess is one."
"Incorrect. The answer is none. Dutch people do not own houses with electricity."
"Because they are poor?"
"Yes."
"That is a very funny joke. I dislike Dutch people."
"Yes, they drive their camping buses incredibly slow along our Autobahn during the summer holidays, thus causing us to brake our BMW's hard."

Baths

I'm not a huge fan of baths. I take one every six years or so but after filling the tub for an hour and sitting in it bored for five minutes, I remember why I rarely take baths. It's like sitting in a really small pool. You can't do laps or lay on a floatie, you just sit there like an idiot staring at your knees wishing you had a cigarette.

Holly likes having baths as she finds them relaxing. Her baths aren't relaxing for me though, as I'm somehow the one responsible for pre-bath preparation. This includes scrubbing the bath, drawing the bath, adding bubble bath, agitating the water, and lighting candles. I did it once for her because I was feeling guilty about something and now it's become expected. Like backrubs.

There's nothing worse than getting into bed, making yourself all comfy, and hearing, "Will you rub my back?"

I usually pretend my arms are too sore from all the bathtub scrubbing and water agitation.

Runaway

I ran away from home when I was five. I didn't like being there and I knew of a much better house where lots of kids lived - a couple of the kids were around my age. I wasn't sure of the address but I knew what the front of the house looked like because I'd seen it dozens of times.

Our house was a place where you had to be quiet and weren't allowed to touch anything. A house of good behaviour. The house I was running away to was full of life and laughter - there was a seesaw in the backyard and the family did fun activities together, such as sack racing. I knew there was a spare bed for me in Peter and Bobby's room because Greg, the oldest brother, had recently moved into the attic.

I only made it four or five blocks before Mr Kostas, our Greek neighbour, drove past and stopped to ask where I was off to and if I wanted a lift. Apparently he didn't watch a lot of television because we drove around for half an hour or so looking for the Brady house before he took me home. Or perhaps he was just humouring me. We did stop to pick up several bags of concrete and some rebar from a hardware store on the way and he told me a story about how his mother used to whip him with an olive tree branch when he got poor grades at school.

Fences

We had a fence put in recently. I wanted a twenty-foot fence, because I shouldn't have to look at our neighbour's shitty yard from our nice yard, but I was told six-feet is the maximum height allowed by law because police officers have to be able to climb over it. Firstly, I don't want police officers climbing over my fence. Secondly, the police officers in our town would be lucky to make it over a knee-high fence. Providing XXXL uniforms is just enabling. Are they tested on their climbing ability or is it just a vague goal?

"Okay cadets, today's test is to see if you can climb over a six-foot fence. Dennis, you're up."
"Are we allowed to use a ladder?"
"Do you have a ladder, Dennis?"
"Yes."
"Well that's fine then. Greg, hold the ladder for Dennis."
"Couldn't we just go through the gate?"
"Sorry, Greg?"
"There's a gate. We could just go through that. It would save mucking about with the ladder."
"Right, I hope everyone else is paying attention because Greg just suggested using the gate. Well done, Greg, police officering isn't just about climbing fences and discounts at Burger King, it's also about improvisation."

Algorithms

Holly and I both have Amazon Prime accounts - I realize it would be cheaper to share one account but there's no way Holly is having access to my purchase history. Even the 'recently viewed items' section would probably mean several uncomfortable chats.

It's not that I'm into anything particularly unusual, it's just that when I search for an item on Amazon, say a book on boat maintenance, it comes up with a 'customers who bought this item also bought' panel and I'm suddenly invested in Jack64's opinion of a 22-foot multi-use ladder with 300-pound rating or Lisa G's review with photos of a toenail clipper.

I don't write the algorithms so don't blame me if it shows men's leotards.

Chores

I have what I guess is considered a weak stomach. If I'm making a sandwich and I discover a piece of bread that has mould on it, I'll dry-retch until the bag of bread is in the trash and out of sight. Even then I'll do mini-gags for several minutes just thinking about how it smelled. Holly usually rolls her eyes while I'm gagging because apparently she grew up in a house made of mould.

A few weeks ago, while I was carrying a garbage bag out to the curb, the bag split and maggots splashed onto my foot. We'd had chicken for dinner three or four days before and there were offcuts in the bag. There was no dry retching or gagging, I instantly projectile vomited onto the sidewalk. It was like a fire hose had been turned on. An old lady jogging past stopped and asked if I was okay and I nodded, pointed to the maggots as explanation, and vomited again. I planned to wash off the sidewalk but when I walked back down the driveway with a hose, the neighbour's cat was eating the vomit/maggot/chicken blend and I vomited a third time.

I made my offspring hose down the sidewalk. He has to earn his keep somehow and he only has three daily chores: Walking the dogs, *taking out the trash*, and being my personal slave.

"Why do I have to hose away your vomit?"
"Because there's maggots and liquidy chicken in it... HurkurkBLEA... See, I almost threw up again just from thinking about it."
"It's your vomit. I'm not hosing it away."
"Yes you are, Seb. It's one of your chores."
"You can't just add chores as you feel like it. Yesterday you added moth catching and cushion fluffing to my chores."
"You let the moth in and the cushion was very flat."
"No it wasn't."
"Yes it was. You should make sure the cushion is fluffed after you use it. For the next person."
"I've never seen you fluff a cushion after you've used it."
"No, because it's your chore. I suppose next you'll be expecting me to Pledge the letterbox for you."
"That's stupid as well. Who cares if the letterbox is shiny? Nobody Pledges their letterbox."
"Fine, let's all move to a trailer in the woods and live like hillbillies then. We'll let in moths and sit on flat cushions and our mailbox can be a milk crate nailed to a stump."
"I'm not hosing away your vomit."
"Yes you are, Seb. If you'd taken out the trash like you're meant to, instead of leaving it for someone else to do, there wouldn't be any vomit to clean up."
"Fine, I'll hose away your vomit... ew, the maggots are still wriggling... HurkurkBLEA."
"Try to only look at it peripherally and not take in any details."

Doubling Down

When my partner Holly and I are arguing, I'll double down rather than admit I'm in the wrong. Sometimes I'll triple or quadruple down. It doesn't matter what the argument is about, we once didn't speak for two days because I wouldn't accept that the blonde girl who plays Piper in *Orange is the New Black* wasn't the same girl from the movie *Clueless*.

Just a few months ago, I ordered a pair of expensive pants online. Nowhere in the description did it state they were 'skinny' and the twelve pleats around the crotch weren't noticeable in the photos. When I tried them on, my lower half looked like a pumpkin stuck on two poles. I intended to return them but forgot and missed the thirty-day window.

When Holly complained that it was a waste of money, I stated that I actually liked the pants a lot and had changed my mind about returning them. They were, in fact, my favourite pants. I wore them to Olive Garden that night - it was Holly's parent's anniversary and they had a $50 gift card. The left leg seam gave out as I climbed into our booth which was quite disappointing as they were the best pants in the world and really it was Holly's fault for making me decide to wear them that night when I'd actually been saving them for a special occasion. I ordered another pair.

French

"It's getting warm outside," the cashier declared, "It will be summer before we know it."

For some reason, I decided the word *indubitably* was an appropriate response but, as I said it, my brain had a mini-stroke and it came out as "Indo bibly bibly."

The cashier stared at me strangely and I decided my only recourse was to pretend I speak another language.

"Bibly albib oobibly."

Remembering a few words from French lessons at school, I also threw in "la pomme" which I think means 'the apple'.

"Will that be all for you today sir?"

"Bibly."

"Your total is $12.98, do you have a store card?"

"Bib."

"Credit or debit?"

"Bebit."

"Would you like the receipt in the bag?"

"Bibly."

"Have a nice day."

"Bib boo."

Stains

When I was about seven, there was an outbreak of Chickenpox in the small Australian country town my family lived in. This was well before a vaccine was developed and around half the kids at school caught it. Nobody wore a mask or social distanced though. If anything, it was the opposite; we were forced by our parents to have sleepovers and attend 'take your shirts off and wrestle with each other' parties.

"Any spots or itching, David?"
"No, why?"
"No reason. Oh, by the way, you're having a sleepover at Matthew's house tonight. It's all been arranged. No need to take your sleeping bag, you can share his bed."
"Matthew has Chickenpox."
"No he hasn't. They're just goosebumps. Give them a good rub tonight to warm Matthew up."

I wasn't a fan of going to Matthew's house. It was a small, two-bedroom home with only a single bathroom, and Matthew's father, Mr Murphy, had killed himself in that bathroom. Apparently he sat in the bathtub, placed the barrel of a loaded rifle in his mouth, and pulled the trigger.

Mrs Murphy was out at the time and Matthew was at school – we were in geography class when the assistant principal knocked on the door and asked to speak to our teacher. They spoke quietly in the hallway for a short time, then Matthew was asked to pack up his stuff.

My mother and Matthew's mother were, if not friends, then something similar. They were members of the local tennis club and met for coffee occasionally. I learned, years later, that Mrs Murphy, who was a hairdresser, had been having an affair with one of her clients, and Mr Murphy found out about it. At the time, however, I was told he'd shot himself because the Australian cricket team lost an important game to England. It was probably the best way my father could come up with to describe a despondency so bad you wanted to die. He really liked cricket and wasn't big on subtlety. Once, when he and my mother decided to have a trial separation and I asked why, he told me that marriage is like a game of cricket, but without an umpire and with only two players, and one is a bitch.

There were times I did visit Matthew's house, but it was reluctantly and I avoided using the bathroom. If I had to urinate, I'd hold one hand up to my face like a horse blinker to block the bathtub from my field of view. I'm not sure what I thought I'd see, but I'd created a scenario in my mind that when Mr Murphy shot himself, his head exploded and brains and blood and eyes and lips splattered everywhere. And that there'd still be evidence of it.

Years before, my father had repaired a leaking toilet cistern at our house and accidentally dropped one of those hockey puck shaped things that turn the water blue onto the floor. Despite the bathroom being scrubbed and bleached many times over the years, the grout between the tiles where the hockey puck thing landed was still stained blue. It was a spot in front of the toilet that you could see between your legs while you were taking a dump. I'd scratch at the grout with a toenail while I was sitting but the colour ran all the way through. At one point, my father scraped out the stained grout and replaced it. The new grout was whiter than the rest and, if anything, stood out worse than the stained grout had. Then, over the space of a few months, the new grout took on a blue tinge.

I imagined that's how it would be with brains and blood and eyes and lips. It wouldn't matter how hard you scrubbed the grout, or how many coats of paint you layered the walls and ceiling with, one day you'd be sitting in the bath and notice everything has a tinge of pink.

Before school one morning, my mother told me to go to Matthew's house that afternoon so Mrs Murphy could give me a haircut. I think it was for a bit of extra cash on the side because I usually went to Barbara's House of Hair & Fridge Magnets for my six-dollar haircuts.

Barbara's House of Hair & Fridge Magnets was originally just called Barbara's House of Hair but at some point

Barbara decided to branch out and start selling art from the salon. At first it was just paintings of her Boston Terrier and Jesus, with a few landscapes of the local area and portraits of clients, but then Barbara tried her hand at Aboriginal art. Barbara wasn't Aboriginal - she was a short, thin, white lady in her seventies with blue rinsed hair - but she managed to create fairly decent dot-based representations of kangaroos and emus on pieces of bark. As our town was off a main tourism road, the paintings practically sold the moment the paint had dried. Discovering she was making a lot more money from the bark paintings than haircuts, Barbara changed the name of her shop to Barbara's House of Hair & Aboriginal Art until a local Aboriginal artist, an actual Aboriginal, took Barbara to court for cultural appropriation and misrepresentation. Barbara agreed to stop forging indigenous artwork and dropped the word Aboriginal from the name of her shop. For a while it was called Barbara's House of Hair & Art, but I guess she sold more hot-glued felt koala fridge magnets than paintings of her Boston Terrier and Jesus, and decided to corner the hair and fridge magnet market.

Often when I was having my hair cut at Barbara's House of Hair & Fridge Magnets, the bell on the door would jingle and tourists would enter looking puzzled and Barbara would say, "Haircut or fridge magnets? If you're looking for Aboriginal art, I have some out back. I can't display it in the front of the shop because the local blackie gets his knickers in a knot."

The 'local blackie', perhaps inspired by Barbara's initial success in the Aboriginal art market, opened his own gallery a few shops down from Barbara's House of Hair & Fridge Magnets. His dot-based kangaroo and emu paintings weren't as good as Barbara's though, and the gallery closed after only six months. It became a café, then a shoe store, and finally a newsagency. There was another newsagency in town so it caused a bit of a turf war; bricks were thrown through windows, rumours were started that the new newsagency owner was a homosexual, and there was even a brawl between the two newsagents at an under-14s football game. Snacks and drinks were thrown and one of the newsagents ripped a windscreen wiper off the other's car and chased him with it. The altercation made front page of the local newspaper and, in the photo they used, Matthew and I could be seen in the background sitting on our bikes. We were pretty much famous for a couple of days and I cut out the photo and had it taped to my bedroom wall until my sister, Leith, obviously jealous, added a voice bubble coming from my head stating, "I'm a girl," because my hair was getting a bit long.

"Hello, Mrs Murphy. Mum told me to come over after school to get a haircut."
"Yes, David, I have it all set up for you. I saw your photo in the newspaper by the way. Very nice."
"Thanks."
"Well, head into the bathroom and we'll get started."
"The bathroom?"

"Yes, it can get a bit messy."
"You could cut my hair outside. It's a nice day."
"Yes, it is, but there's no plug outside for the clippers."
"You could run an extension cord out there."
"Don't be silly, come along. I've put a kitchen chair in the bathtub for you to sit on."

Mr Murphy had worked for the Australian Parks & Wildlife Service, it's why he owned a rifle I suppose. He also drove a white government-issued Land Cruiser with four-wheel drive. As such, there were plenty of secluded spots in the Australian outback he could have driven to and shot himself. Maybe it was a spur of the moment decision, or maybe he wanted to stain the grout, to make a statement that couldn't be scrubbed away.

It had been though. There were no remnants of brains and blood and eyes and lips on the bathroom tiles, no pink tinge. The tiles and grout were sparkling clean, as if new - as if it had never happened. I'd feared something that wasn't there, blinkered myself and drawn out that fear far longer than was necessary. Once when I'd needed to poo, I ran home to do it and shit myself on the way.

Cargo Shorts

I'm a big fan of cargo shorts. I get a bit of flack for wearing them but I'll choose six handy pockets over being fashionable any day of the week. I wore cargo shorts to a wedding once. I ironed them though.

I honestly believe the world would be a much happier place if everyone suddenly decided, "Six handy pockets. I get it now. I'm never wearing anything else again."

The saddest day of each year for me is when I leave the house in cargo shorts and realize my legs are cold. It's all downhill from there and I have to search for trousers in the back of the wardrobe. I realize cargo shorts also come in pant length but I wouldn't be seen dead wearing cargo pants in public. I know a guy named Nick who wears cargo pants and he shoots pumpkins behind his trailer with an AR-15 semi-automatic rifle.

Maps

Once, during a family road trip across Australia, my father drove six hundred miles in the wrong direction and blamed my mother for folding the roadmap wrong.

"You have to fold it in the middle, then over, then across twice... no wait... over, then over again, then across twice, then over again."
"What does it matter?"
"The creases go the wrong way if you don't fold it properly."
"Why don't you just admit you missed the turnoff?"
"It was in a crease. Facing the wrong way."

Mr Steve

I've killed two animals in my life. The first was a kangaroo that I struck while driving Seb to school several years ago. It's a common misconception that kangaroos plague Australian city streets but they do occasionally make their way into residential areas. Their numbers are similar to that of deer in the United States but deer don't bound twenty feet into the air. I've had to brake for deer a few times but you are not given that opportunity with kangaroos, they just kind of appear from above in front of you. The car was a complete writeoff. We thought the kangaroo was fine at first, as it got up and took a few wobbly hops, but then it leant back, wiggled its arms like Neo dodging bullets in the Matrix, and keeled over. Seb poked it with a stick and took a picture on his phone for Show & Tell.

The second animal I killed was a hamster named Mr Steve. I was vacuuming under Seb's bed and heard the 'thok' as something went up but I didn't realise what it was until I reversed the hose to clear the blockage. There was another 'thok' followed by a 'thud' as Mr Steve hit the wall. I was equally horrified and impressed by the distance cleared. I put him back in his cage for Seb to find later and suggested dysentery, due to the state off Seb's bedroom, as the most likely cause of death.

AT&T

Holly's parents, Marie and Tom, got their first smart phones last week. Now they're like teenagers, never looking up from their phones except to make statements of wonder such as, "Oh my god, does your phone have a calculator on it? Mine does. Look."

Marie even went into her settings last night and now she has a photo of Donald Trump playing golf as her background. She tried to show Tom how to do it but somehow reset his phone to factory settings and he had to go back to AT&T.

A teenage girl behind the counter told him there was a two-hour wait and he yelled at her and was asked to leave. He says he's going to switch over to Verizon.

Man Cave

When I was young, our house had an attached garage that had been converted into a 'granny-flat' for my mother's sister, Auntie Brenda, to stay in after she became terminally ill. It wasn't much of a conversion, my father did the work himself, but it had a bed and basic amenities.

My father was originally against the conversion. He and Auntie Brenda had physically scuffled once during a family Christmas dinner after he called her a "disgusting bushpig" for chewing with her mouth open, and she spat a mouthful of stuffing and cranberry sauce at his face in response. His favorite white Lacoste polo shirt was ruined. He sent Auntie Brenda an invoice for replacement, with follow-up reminders and a final notice, but she never paid it.

The conversion only went ahead after my mother agreed it could become a man-cave after Auntie Brenda died. My father bought a framed print of dogs playing poker and a neon beer clock in anticipation.

Auntie Brenda was originally given six months to live but lasted three years. I'm not sure what her illness was but she lost her hair and coughed a lot. Often she'd cough until she soiled herself and there was a special basket in our laundry for her bedding with an airtight lid. Sometimes my sister would remove the basket lid and lock me in the laundry. Once, she threw a used adult diaper at me and urine went in my mouth. Which isn't relative to the story in any way, I just want it on record. I've not mentioned the incident since as I'm waiting for the right moment.

"David, the doctors have given me less than two weeks to live if I don't find a donor kidney match. I know it's a big ask but, as my brother, I was wondering..."
"Remember when you threw a used adult diaper at me?"
"What?"
"Urine went in my mouth. Auntie Brenda's urine."
"Okay..."
"It was quite upsetting at the time. I thought it meant I had whatever she had. I wrote a will."
"I don't..."
"Something to think about as your dialysis machine fails and you convulse to death."

As she was bedridden, we didn't see much of Auntie Brenda but we heard her often. During particularly bad coughing fits, my father would pound on the adjoining wall and yell, "I'm trying to watch TV in here, just fucking die already!" and she'd yell back, "Fuck you, monkey!" - a reference to my father's long sideburns. He shaved the sideburns off the day after she died so I suspect the name bothered him only slightly less than having Auntie Brenda know it bothered him at all.

I remember the evening Auntie Brenda died, we were watching *Magnum PI* and my father said, "Haven't heard Gollum hacking up a lung in a while, better go and check on her, David."

She was naked, hanging half off the bed, a large, wet fecal stain beneath her hips. I'd never seen naked breasts before so I gave one a squeeze.

I'm joking about squeezing Auntie Brenda's breast. I wasn't even the one who discovered her. I only added that paragraph because I imagined the look on Holly's face as she proofreads it. I'll delete it before this book goes to print unless I forget or it messes up my formatting, otherwise I'll receive dozens of annoying emails from old people - angry at the world about their shingles and the price of irritable bowel medicine - asking what, exactly, is amusing about molesting a dead relative.

It was my sister who checked on Auntie Brenda. She had nightmares for years afterwards and refused to go into the converted garage even after my father took the bed to the dump and put a bar, television, dart board, and two beanbags in there.

For a while, there was a poster behind the bar of Kelly LeBrock sitting on a moped in a bikini, but my mother ripped it down during an argument about having her sewing table and chair in the man cave.

"Why can't it be the 'family cave'?"
"We already have a family cave, it's called the living room. This is my area to get away from everyone."
"Well perhaps I'd like my own area to get away from everyone as well."
"You already have one."
"Where?"
"The kitchen."
"..."
"You're welcome to visit though."

A few days after the argument, while my mother was at the supermarket, my father cleaned out the tool shed, ran an extension cord from the house, and put her sewing table and chair in there. He also put a piece of green carpet on the concrete floor and hung a painting of two kittens playing with yarn on a wall.

I'm sure he expected my mother to be delighted but, after being led outside in a blindfold for the reveal, she locked herself in the bathroom and cried.

Greenpeace

I dated an environmental activist once. At least I thought we were dating. Her name was Yolanda, which is apparently Polish for 'the unwashed'. We spent 48 hours chained to a tree on a housing development, then she informed me she was a lesbian and had just needed a ride.

It's not easy getting a refund for Greenpeace membership. I had to ring my bank and dispute the credit card charge. I did get to keep the T-shirt though. Really, I deserved it for everything I'd done for the environment. There was a lot of sap on that tree.

Vaping

I know a guy named Brandon who vapes. He only owns one shirt. I don't know him well but we do the tight lipped smile and nod when we see each other at events and he invited me to his wedding recently. I didn't go because it was a *Harry Potter* themed wedding and guests had to bring their own wands.

Brandon convinced me to try his vape once, it was a coffee-menthol-hibiscus blend that he'd mixed himself and called *Mistvana*. I assume he has a special spot in his kitchen with dozens of little vape-oil bottles that he mixes and tries and nods and says to himself, "It's more of an art than a science."

"Rachel, try this blend…"
"Okay… hmm… it's very *coconutty*."
"Yes, I used coconut as the base, but can you identify the other flavours?"
"Mint and pomegranate?"
"No, despondency and self-disgust.

Blue Eyeshadow

I believed in a God up until I was about five. The westernised version, not the Chinese wind and soup Gods or the Roman sea and lightning ones. I remember kneeling by my bed, hands clasped, begging God to give me a Spirograph. They were advertised on television in the late seventies and I'd decided I was going to be a professional spirographologist.

Children are easily indoctrinated; if you could avoid outside influences and you were a bit of dick, you could easily produce an adult that 'knows' we are made of malleable rocks and came from the planet Scotchtape in a rocket made out of whipped cream. Even *with* outside influences, it's easy to indoctrinate a child using a reward system or punishment. I believed in Santa and the tooth fairy because there were presents and cash involved. I believed in a God because if I didn't, I was ten times more likely to be hit by a car while riding my bike or become a homosexual.

My grandmother was the one who told me that. She was a narrow-minded woman who hated Arabs, atheists, Jews, homosexuals, men with beards, Asians, women who wore eyeshadow, and Indians. Indians from India, not Native American Indians - though she probably hated them as well. She once told me that 'people like us' have white skin because

God created us from the purest clay, and that Indians have dark skin because they were created out of poo. That's why they smell bad and are poor.

My grandmother's bible was about the size of a toaster oven, with several hundred sticky notes poking out the sides making the volume even thicker. Many of the sticky notes were colour-coded, with yellow referencing passages that justified intolerance, blue referencing those who should be stoned to death, and pink referencing passages that came in handy whenever she needed to make anyone feel bad about themselves. A lot of the sticky notes had names written on them and why the passage was appropriate, for example: *Cheryl Phillips - blue eyeshadow* marked a passage about sexual immorality, and *David Thorne - sultanas* was attached to a passage about thieves and swindlers; I'd once lied about eating a box of sultanas my grandmother was planning to use in a fruit cake.

It was the story about Noah's Ark that first sparked my doubt in theological accuracy. I couldn't get a straight answer on the actual size of the boat, just that it was 'really big' and when I pressed my grandmother on the logistics of fitting two of every animal - and all the supplies they'd require - on even a 'really big' boat, she changed the whole story and informed me that God shrunk the animals to the size of mice as they entered the ark, then made them full-sized again when they departed.

It was at that moment I realized my grandmother was just making shit up as she went along. Indians weren't made out of poo, millions of animals can't fit on a boat, and God doesn't give a fuck if Cheryl Phillips wears blue eyeshadow.

Cheryl Phillips was my grandmother's neighbour. She had a Saint Bernard named Harry and once when I jumped the fence to play with the dog, Cheryl asked if I wanted to take Harry for a walk. We strolled around the block with Harry on a leash and it became a regular thing after that. This was a few years before my family got a dog and I grew quite attached to Harry. At some point, Cheryl hurt her foot and had to wear a big boot so she paid me to walk Harry after school. I would have done it for free but she insisted. It was technically my first job and, with the money I earned, I bought a Spirograph. God wasn't going to bring me one and when I'd asked my parents, my father said, "I'm not wasting money on wiggly circles. Just trace around a cup."

When Harry died - I think he had cancer - I helped Cheryl bury him in her backyard. We had to dig a pretty big hole, Saint Bernards aren't lap dogs, and it took a few hours. After the dirt had been patted down, Cheryl held my hand and we stood there looking at the mound.

"What happens to him now?" I asked.
"Worms eat him," Cheryl said, "then birds eat the worms and feed their babies with them and Harry becomes a part of all the other animals in the world. That's his job now."

"He doesn't go to Heaven?"
"Do you think he goes to Heaven?"
"No, there's no such thing."
"No, but it's nicer that way. It makes the time we shared more valuable."

I've no idea what my grandmother died of. Apparently she was standing in her kitchen, washing dishes, and simply dropped dead. Perhaps it was an overload of distain. Years later, while helping my sister clean out her garage, I discovered my grandmother's bible in a cardboard box. It wasn't as large as I remembered but it took me two hands to lift and carry it to my car. At home, I removed the sticky notes, tore out several pages that had handwritten notes, put everything in a garbage bag, and threw it out with the rest of the trash.

Method Acting

I read somewhere that during the filming of *My Left Foot*, Daniel Day-Lewis stayed in character for his portrayal of a wheelchair-bound person for the entire shooting schedule. Ccrew members had to feed him, carry him to and from set, and help him use the bathroom. If I were one of the crewmembers and my boss said, "David, I'm going to need you to wipe Daniel's arse because he's pretending he can't do it himself," I'd resign. On the way out, I'd remind Daniel Day-Lewis that Robert Downey Jr. makes forty times what he does for superhero movies. I haven't seen *My Left Foot*, because I don't watch movies about feet, but from what I can tell it's about a guy in a wheelchair who can move his left foot. I can move both my feet and nobody has approached me about the movie rights.

"So, David, we received your script titled *My Left and Right Foot and My Legs and Both My Arms and Hands*, but we're a little confused by the plot. It's about a man who has full working use of all his limbs?"
"That's right. He's perfectly fine."
"Okay. Does he have any special abilities or talents?"
"No, not really. He can draw a little bit."
"Oh, portraits and the like?"
"No, just cats and stuff."

Gossip

It began in the small village of Harrisonburg, Virginia, but, like an airborne super-virus with no known cure, it spread rapidly. Within minutes it was in Chicago, hours later there were reports that it had spread to New York, Los Angeles, Mexico City, London, Sydney...

Jack O'Reilly had no contact with the outside world. He lived off the grid, in a small log cabin by a river, on a heavily forested property his great, great grandfather had hunted on. The nearest town was a ten-day trek away and it had been almost twenty years since he'd last had human contact. He had no need or desire for modern technologies; he made his own lamps from beaver fat and the forest provided wood for the stove and meat for his belly. There were large bass in the river and that morning, he'd risen at first light and made his way down a well-worn trail with his fishing rod. He sat on the edge of the bank and cast his line... A canoe came around the bend and a lone paddler waved frantically.

"Hello? Jack?" Lori yelled to him, "Seb spent all of his money on computer parts and is flying to America broke. I just thought you should know."

Seven Seconds

While having lunch at work today, my coworker Ben stated, "If a fly lands on your food, you have to count to seven before shooing it away."

His logic behind this is apparently based on how flies eat: When a fly lands on food, it vomits on it, waits for the vomit to dissolve the food, then sucks the vomit and the dissolved food back up with some kind of straw thing on its face. Shooing away the fly before it sucks back up the vomit and dissolved food means you eat the fly's vomit.

"So you just let flies sit on your food?"
"For seven seconds, yes."
"Do you use a timer or count in your head?"
"I use the hippopotamus method. One hippopotamus, two hippopotamus etcetera. It's more exact than the Mississippi method. When you say Mississippi, it's easy to run the syllables together. You can't do that with hippopotamus."
"Sure. Technically it would be 'one hippopotamus, two hippopotamuses though. That's an extra syllable."
"I'm not counting hippopotamuses, I'm just using the word hippopotamus between the numbers as a timer. Besides, if I were counting hippopotamuses, I'd use hippopotami which has the same amount of syllables."

"Do you continue eating while you count or wait patiently for the fly to finish?"

"It depends on the food. If it's a proper dinner and a fly lands on the mashed potatoes, I'll eat some carrots or peas while it finishes. If it's a sandwich, obviously I'd have to wait the full seven seconds."

"That's assuming all flies take exactly seven seconds to eat. You might get a particularly ravenous one who finishes in six seconds. Which could mean eating a second round of vomit."

"No, they all take exactly seven seconds. They have a built-in clock. Like cicadas."

Lawn

Greek people like concrete. Concreting their front lawn and adding columns doesn't make their suburban three-bedroom brick house the Parthenon, but it's a symbol of status to Greek people - the more columns, ponds and statues in their yard, the higher their social ranking. For everyone else living on the street, it's an eyesore that should be bulldozed. We had a lot of Greeks in our neighborhood when I was a kid. Our next-door neighbour Mr Kostas was Greek and his perpetual concrete-based landscaping infuriated my father.

"Give it a fucking rest, Dennis! You can't run a cement mixer after 7pm. It's a city ordinance."
"Fuck you, Philip!"
"No, fuck you, Dennis. I'll call the cops."
"If you call the cops on me, you call the cops on my whole family."
"You're not the Godfather, Dennis."
"The Kostas are well respected in the community."
"Not around here, dickhead. We all think your front yard looks like shit."
"My front yard is beautiful. Your front yard looks like shit."
"At least I've got lawn, Dennis. Lawn!"

Television

A television is always on in our house somewhere. I'm not even sure how many sets we have but going by last month's cable bill, I'd say eight or nine hundred. Too much television is apparently bad for you but we balance the junk we watch with educational programs such as *Jeopardy* and... well, just *Jeopardy* actually. Maybe *Shark Week* every year, that's educational. I only watch it for the seal attacks though, I couldn't care less about boat-hippies in Speedo's discussing graphs that show shark feeding territories have decreased in the last eighteen months due to overfishing. Decrease it to one spot. I'd be fine with going to the beach if I could say, "Here's a nice place to swim, not over there though, that's the shark spot."

I know a couple, who aren't homeless, that don't own a single television set. Not even one in their bathroom. I won't visit them as it means having to look at each other and come up with things to say. Things other than, "Why don't you have a television set?"

I get the whole, "We'd rather develop our minds" argument, but it's undermined when the people saying it would tie for second place in a 'who's the least interesting' competition' because having a winner would be too interesting.

"Did you watch *The Handmaid's Tale* last night?"
"No, we don't own a television."
"Oh my god. Are you poor?"
"No, we choose not to have one."
"Do you own chairs?"
"Yes, of course."
"What do you face them at? Are they all just facing in random directions?"
"No, they're facing each other. To allow for conversation."
"Oh my god, what do you talk about?"
"Many things. From 'how our day went' to political and social issues, the economy, arts, spirituality, climate change, nature, science…"
"Every night? It doesn't get exhausting after three or four times?"
"No, last night, my wife and I practiced our throat singing. We're now able to produce three, sometimes four, pitches simultaneously. We start with a low drone then, by subtle manipulations of our vocal tracts, we break up the sound, amplifying one or more overtones until they can be heard as additional pitches while the drone continues at a lower volume. Would you like to hear some?"
"No thank you."

Our neighbours, Carl and Toni, also don't own a television and, as Carl's only hobbies are mowing his lawn and loving Jesus, I imagine their evenings are spent sitting in chairs reading Bible passages waiting to die.

"Did you say something, Carl?"

"No, I just swallowed loudly."

"Ah."

"Yes, I decided to swallow my candy rather than wait until it was sucked small enough to disappear. These new caramel apple filled Werther's aren't as good as the originals. We should have kept the receipt so I could staple it to my complaint letter to Mr Werther."

"Yes, Dear... so.... I noticed the Harrison's at number 98 bought a new television. The box was out with their bins on collection day. It's a Samsung. A HD one apparently."

"The only HD we need is the Higher Deity, Toni."

"Yes. Of course."

"I can't wait to meet Jesus. Did you know he has an army of angels and they all have flaming swords?"

"He has?"

"Yes. Well, not all of the angels have swords of course, some prefer harps. Mainly the girl angels. Because you need long fingernails to pluck the strings. "

"That makes sense."

"Plus, there's the servant angels."

"Servant angels?"

"Yes, if you want a Werther's, poof, an angel appears and gives you one. You don't even have to ask, you just have to think about it and they pop up. Of the original Werther's of course, not these. Everyone's telepathic in Heaven."

"Really? I'm not sure how I'd feel about everyone knowing what I'm thinking."

"Nobody cares what you're thinking, Toni."

Karaoke

My friend Ross visited from Australia recently. We did the tourist things, shot guns, and rode a pig. We also took a range of illegal substances because Ross has an ongoing challenge with himself to see how much, and how many, foreign substances his body can handle without dying.

During one of our outings, we came across a small bar in the middle of nowhere. The clientele were in their sixties or older, nursing pints and smoking cigarettes at tables pocked with scorch marks. The interior was dimly lit by neon Coors Lite and Pabst Blue Ribbon signs and, on a small stage towards the back, an old lady wearing a hair net was belting out Dolly Parton's *Jolene*.

"Oooh. Karaoke! We're definitely doing that."
"Really, Ross?"
"Yes, after I've finished my beer. You're not going to sing?"
"No, I don't know any farm emo songs and I'll probably be lynched if I sing anything else."
"Well, Holly will do karaoke with me, won't you Holly."
"No."
"Weak. Do you think anyone will care if I do a line of coke here or should I go to the bathroom?"
"Probably best to keep it low key."

Hair net lady followed up *Jolene* with another three or four Dolly Parton songs, and Ross got a bit annoyed and said that there should be a limit on how many songs you can sing before it's someone else's turn. Nobody else seemed to mind though, they clapped and yelled, "Sing another one, Hair Net Lady!" They didn't actually call her Hair Net Lady but I can't remember what her name was. The moment Hair Net Lady exhausted the Dolly Parton playlist and sat down, Ross leapt to the stage. He flicked through the list of songs available, frowned, then shrugged and made a selection. The opening chords to *Don't You Want Me* by The Human League flooded the bar. A couple of patrons looked up from their beers and frowned, but a woman wearing a bedazzled denim jacket screeched, "Ooh, I love this song!"

Pleased by the positive reaction to his song choice, Ross opened with, 'Okay, this one goes out to the lady with the denim jacket," and amended the lyrics to, "You were wearing a denim jacket in a smoky dark bar, when I met you…"

His tonal range wasn't great but Ross received a decent amount of applause. Mostly from Holly and I, but denim jacket lady chipped in and gave him one of those whistles some people can do with their fingers. Nobody yelled, "Sing another one, Beard Boy!" but he did anyway. Mid-way through the murder of Soft Cell's *Tainted Love*, Holly turned to me and said, "That actually looks like fun."
"You should have a go then," I told her.
"Maybe," Holly nodded.

Holly had never sung karaoke before. She hummed and hawed about doing it, you could tell she wanted to, but after Ross relinquished the stage, it remained empty.

"Nobody wants to follow that," Ross said, wiping sweat from his face, "pretty good huh?"
"Yes," I replied, "very impressive bitonal range. Holly wants to have a go but she's too nervous."
"Really?" Ross searched in a jacket pocket and took out a small plastic bag. Peeking inside, he selected a pill and dropped it into Holly's beer. "Drink up," he said.
"What is it? Holly asked.
"Magic," Ross replied, "It will turn you into the best singer in the world. I'm going to have another go while it kicks in. Any requests? No? I might ask denim jacket lady if she wants to do a duet then."

For the record, I should probably note that Holly doesn't usually take drugs. She might have the occasional puff of a joint if offered, but she doesn't smoke crack or inject heroin into her eyeballs. She also doesn't usually throw back drinks containing magic pills. Ross has a way of normalizing drugs though, and he'd taken four himself earlier and hadn't died.

"What the fuck is an island in a stream?" Holly asked, "Do they mean stepping stones?"
"Probably. You feeling all right?"
"Yes, I feel great. Definitely down for a bit of karaoke when these two are done singing about rocks."

Holly's karaoke debut was, well, I've never seen anything like it so I lack an appropriate adjective. Perhaps a combination of the adjectives spectacular, frightening, and energetic. Holly's karaoke debut was spightetic. The regulars at the bar certainly hadn't seen anything quite so spightetic, they've likely not since. Not only did Holly know every word to *No Sleep Till Brooklyn* by the Beastie Boys, she knew all the moves as well. She hipped and hopped and wopped and spighteticized all over the stage, throwing gangsta signs and cold kickin' it live.

Ross missed most of the performance because he was in the bathroom with denim jacket lady, but he caught the tail end where Holly did a Patrick Swayze knee slide across the stage and dropped the mike. The bar was silent for a long moment. Then erupted in applause.

That was pretty much it for Holly, she was now ready to quit her day job and become a professional karaoke singer. She owned the stage until 2am when the bar closed, and ordered a karaoke machine on Amazon at 2.15am. Not just any karaoke machine either, it has a fuckzillion watts, a thirty-foot subwoofer, and laser lights that will take out a retina. It's also portable. This means Holly can take it anywhere. And she does.

"So the funeral is at 1pm, followed by a small gathering of twenty or so people at my house."
"Ooh, should I bring my karaoke machine?"

Locks

I lock the doors when I'm home because Holly's father, Tom, once poked his head into the bathroom while I was in the shower and said, "Just dropping off a watermelon."

Years ago, after visiting my friend Geoffrey at his house, I realized I'd left my sunglasses behind and went back to get them. I'd only been gone a few minutes, so I walked straight in without knocking and discovered Geoffrey taking a dump in his kitchen trashcan.

It was one of those trashcans with the flip up lid and Geoffrey was squatting over it, naked from the waist down, pressing the foot pedal down with his hand. As he yelled and leapt up in surprise, the lid closed and a half-out log broke off and landed on top.

Nothing prepares you for this kind of social interaction so I stood there staring at the poo on the lid while Geoffrey screamed at me for not knocking. Apparently the plumbing in his toilet wasn't working or something but who shits in a trashcan? Shit in the shower and waffle-stomp those nuggets down the drain like the rest of us.

Rednecks

Rednecks used to be entertaining. They struck oil and moved to Beverly Hills and jumped cars over creeks. They were good ol' boys, never meanin' no harm. You couldn't pitch television shows like that these days.

"So it's about two rednecks who drive around in an orange car with a confederate flag painted on the roof?"
"Yes, and they have compound bows that shoot arrows with explosives on them."
"Right. Does the car need to have the confederate flag on it?"
"Yes, that's how you know they're rednecks."
"It's just that it's a bit of a touchy subject. We'd be alienating a majority of the American viewing public."
"It's history, not hate."
"Sure. So they just drive around and shoot things with explosive arrows?"
"No, of course not. They have adventures."
"Oh, okay. That sounds fun. What kind of adventures?"
"Beating up faggots and niggers."
"Sorry, what?"
"Foiling bank robberies and saving orphanages."

Fat Dog

Our dog Laika is really fat. I refuse to be seen in public with her because people point and shake their heads and I can tell they're thinking I'm a bad dog owner and probably force-feeding the poor thing. Laika looks like a barrel with thin sticks sticking out the bottom and the size of her body makes her head look tiny. I'll try drawing her so you can get a better idea...

You may be thinking, 'Oh David, don't be silly, obviously you've exaggerated the size of Laika's body for comedic purposes', but it's actually an incredibly accurate likeness and I'm considering entering it in this year's Archibold Prize. Once, while chasing a thrown stick, Laika tripped and rolled down a hill. It was like the scene in that movie where Han Solo finds a gold monkey in a cave. If she were human, her name would be Louise and her hobbies would include blocking exits, cake, and writing formal complaints.

Judgmental

We moved recently, to get away from our neighbor Carl, and our new neighbours are a dwarf and his blurry wife. He might not actually be a dwarf, it's possible he's just really short with weird chubby arms and legs. And his wife isn't really blurry, just so nondescript that ten seconds after seeing her, I forget what she looks like. I think she has straight brown hair. Also, her name might be Karen. Or Jill. I don't care. Apparently they're artists but I've known artists who are capable of using a weed whacker. It's not all just about wearing black and bringing rusty benches home from the dump to put on your front lawn. A rusty dump-bench doesn't say, "Look at how bohemian we are", it says, "Fuck you, we're taking everyone's property value down with us."

The crackhouse-chique theme isn't restrained to the exterior either; Dwarf and Blurry don't own blinds so at night, we get the full experience of what it would be like to live in a third-world country. At some point, one of them must have declared, "You know what would make great living room furniture? A beige plastic outdoor setting from Wal-Mart. And I'll paint it without primer." To which the other no doubt answered, "Good idea, it will go perfectly with our cinder-block bookcase and the six-foot papier-mâché giraffe we found in a dumpster behind Pier-1."

Also, I once saw the blurry wife dancing in a poncho while the dwarf played bongos. It must have been a bongo song about birds because she was flapping her poncho like wings. It's easy to be judgmental though. Really easy. I'd probably still bother if it took effort however. I'd have nothing to talk about otherwise.

"I see your neighbors put a bench on their front lawn."
"Yes, a metal one. Looks great."
"Really, David?"
"Yes, it's very bohemian. They're artists, did you know?"
"It's covered in rust."
"Ah, yes, the patina. So much character."
"It's an eyesore. And weird. Who puts an old rusty bench in the middle of their front lawn facing the street? Are they going to sit on it and wave to people passing by?"
"I do hope so. The neighborly wave is sadly uncommon nowadays."
"You're behaving rather oddly and there's a large vein on your forehead that looks like it's about to burst."
"Yes, I'm having a stroke."

Holly and I actually play a game called 'The Judgmental Game' which we made up and somehow don't feel bad about. Basically, if you're driving along and you see someone wearing, for example, terry toweling, you declare, "Hey, there's Terry!" and the other person has to guess Terry's last name - which in this instance is obviously Toweling. Just this afternoon, on the way to the supermarket, we passed Roger

Redpants and argued whether Erin Electric Scooter counts because it was a bit of a stretch. Holly's not very good at the game.

"Hey, there's Sally!"
"Hmm... Sally who?"
"Sally Shopping Cart."
"We all have shopping carts, Holly. We're shopping in a supermarket."
"And? Hey, there's Sue!"
"Sue Shopping Cart?"
"No, Sue Williams. I went to school with her sister."

Sorry Bradley Died

When I was about ten, my route to school passed a property with an orange tree growing in the front garden. Walking at a slow pace one morning - so as not close the fifty foot gap between myself and Bradley McPherson the school bully - I watched Bradley pluck an orange, turn, and throw it at me.

If I'd stood my ground, the orange would have struck my chest but instead, ducking and turning, it exploded against the left side of my head.

A few weeks later, I lost hearing in my left ear and, shortly after, experienced earaches. Following a visit to the doctor, it was discovered that pulp had imbedded itself deep within my ear canal and an orange seed had sprouted. When they pulled it out, the roots were almost two inches long.

Bradley McPherson was hit and killed by a car shortly after while furiously peddling his Malvern Star across a K-Mart carpark pursued by store detectives. When a card for his parents was passed around the classroom for everybody to sign, I wrote, "Sorry Bradley died" using an orange pen and coloured in the O solid. I also drew a picture of Bradley riding his bike with a giant snake chasing him

Listening Skills

A few years back, the agency I worked for was commissioned to design a brochure titled *Living with Anxiety*. Along with the standard breathing and physical exercises, it described a Japanese technique called *Iwa-Baransu* which requires you to close your eyes and visualise balancing a round stone on top of slightly larger round stone to form a stack against a wind. The wind's strength is determined by the issue at hand. Apparently it was a technique practiced by Samurai before battle and now more commonly before business meetings.

I tried it prior to a meeting to discuss responsibility for twenty-thousand copies of the brochure being printed and sent out with 'We'll bring highkicks' listed under services offered instead of 'Well-being checkups', and have used the technique daily since.

"Are you falling asleep?"
"No Holly, tell me more about your day."
"Well, I returned her call and left a second message and she called me back an hour later while I was at lunch and left a message to call her but when I did, it went straight to messages again. As far as I'm concerned, the bitch can order her own promotional travel-mugs."

The Spot

The River Murray is Australia's longest river, winding its way through two-thousand miles of the outback before reaching the ocean. It saw substantial commercial use by paddle-steamers during the 1900s and the river is dotted with small towns that once supported industry. These towns cater to families on holidays and retirees now, shoreline stores that once supplied grain and coal sell ice-cream and inflatable rafts. The retirees mainly live on houseboats, it's a very popular thing for retirees to do. Selling your house and buying a houseboat to live on when you reach sixty-five is South Australia's equivalent of 'moving to a condo in Florida'. I suppose it's the freedom that draws them, being able to cruise anywhere they want, finding a quiet area and docking for a few weeks, then moving on. Most of them just stay parked in the towns though, probably for the television reception.

My father liked the river. He didn't fish or own a boat but he liked sitting beside the river drinking beer. It took a couple of hours to drive to his favourite spot, another hour or so to set up camp, then he would sit by the river and drink beer until it was time to pack up and leave. There were closer camping spots, places we could have driven to in half the time, but my father hated anyone camping within twenty miles of us. He also hated houseboats cruising past and regularly commented that he, "didn't come out here to wave at old cunts." When houseboats did occasionally pass by, the retirees would wave and my father would yell at them to fuck off. Once, a houseboat parked directly across from us under cliffs and my father paddled out to it on an inflatable raft and told an elderly couple that if they stayed where they were, he was going to paddle back out in the middle of night while they were sleeping, douse the boat in petrol, and set it alight. They left threatening that they were going to report him to the police when they got to the next town but the river police didn't pay us a visit. Not that time. The next time we went to the river, my father took a few dozen signs that he'd had printed stating, 'No Houseboats' and made me paddle up and down the river, both sides, nailing them to trees. The next day, the river police made me take them back down.

It was a nice spot, thirty or so miles from a small town called Morgan. There were cliffs on one side, which caught the afternoon sun and shone red, with ledges that we could paddle over to and climb. There was no way of getting to the top but there were several outcrops that we could get to and jump off. My father made a rope swing one year but it snapped on the first go and I broke my arm and three ribs. I should have let my sister go first.

On the side of the river we camped on, there was a small sandy beach with a flat area above where we pitched our tent.

It was a large canvas tent, big enough for four people to sleep in plus room for our gear. My father made a flag for the tent once; it featured two crossed beer bottles and the words, River Rat Lodge. He attached it to the top of the tent with a gum-tree branch and duct tape but it disappeared during a windy night. He made my sister and I walk around the area for a couple of hours looking for it but it was nowhere to be found. I discovered, years later, that my mother had taken it down and thrown it into the river because it was embarrassing.

It had been my father's favourite spot for as long as I can remember. There were photos of me as a baby there. One showed me on my father's knee as he sat by the river drinking beer. He had long sideburns and was wearing an orange tank top and tiny mint-green tennis shorts with a belt. I was wearing his aviator sunglasses and had a cigarette in my mouth. Another, as a toddler, showed me screaming with a turtle attached to my left foot. I assume my father grabbed the camera and took the shot before helping me, which may have contributed to me losing my small toe.

To get to the spot, we had to turn onto an unmarked dirt track and pass through three old cattle gates. The gates were rusty and never closed, the second having fallen off its hinges long ago. One day, as we headed to the river for a long-weekend, the last gate was chained and padlocked. An old car hood was leaning against it with the words For Sale and a telephone number spray-painted across it.

It took a few months of negotiations for my father to purchase the property. The land for sale totalled three-hundred acres but all my father wanted was 'his spot' so the owner agreed to subdivide and sell him ten acres out of the parcel.

We went to the river a lot more often after that - every weekend in summer. We'd leave Friday afternoon after my father got home from work and get back late Sunday. One weekend, my father hired a trailer and towed building materials to construct an eight-metre floating dock. We used it to tie up a couple of kayaks and my sister and I would run along it and jump off into the water. It became his new favourite place to sit and drink beer. He added to it over the years and it became a kind of patio, with a covered shade cloth and a table and chairs. A truck of sand was brought in to extend the beach and when my father bought a speedboat, a ramp was added to back it into the water and then a small shed to house equipment and toys. We had tubes, kneeboards and a giant banana and water sports became one of the key aspects of being there. Sometimes I was allowed to invite a school friend to come up for the weekend but only one at a time as there wasn't room in the tent for more, and, as my father didn't like anyone knowing where 'the spot' was, he'd make them put on a blind-fold just before the turnoff. A few years before, my parents had invited Mr and Mrs Ellis, a family from their tennis club, up for a four-day weekend. They'd chatted and it turned out the Ellis family enjoyed camping and had all their own equipment. The plan was for our family to drive up Thursday night with the Ellis family joining us the next day around noon. My father drew them a detailed 'mud map' showing how to get there. On Friday morning, my father had me clear a flattish area in camp so the Ellis family would have a place to pitch their tent when they arrived. There were quite a few rocks so he'd packed a pickaxe.

"Dad, my arms are getting tired."
"Would you like some cheese with that whine?"*
"No."
"I can still see bumps. You know how the Egyptians got their land so level for building on?"
"How?"
"They flooded it with water. Whatever stuck out of the water, they'd dig away."
"You want me to pour water on it?"
"No, don't be stupid. Why would the Ellis family want to pitch a tent in mud?"

My efforts were wasted as Mr and Mrs Ellis decided it would be a much better idea to leave their vehicle in Morgan, rent a houseboat, and cruise down to 'the spot' to park and stay for the three nights.

---

* *"Would you like some cheese with that whine" was one of my father's favourite responses to complaints. He also liked, "Should I call you a wahbulance?", "You'd better pick up that bottom lip before someone trips over it", "Come here and I'll give you something to cry about" and, "Bitch somewhere else, I'm trying to watch the cricket."*

My father was sitting at the edge of the river drinking beer when the houseboat came into view and slowed. He yelled at it to fuck off and threw an empty beer bottle, striking the hull, before realising who it was. It was the first time Mr Ellis had driven a houseboat and it was his first time pulling into shore. He powered up and headed straight for where my father was sitting, forcing my father to leap out of his chair and run as the houseboat's twin hulls plowed their way several feet up the beach. My father's chair went under the left hull. It was a folding camp chair that he'd bought himself for his birthday a few days before, blue with his favourite football team's logo on the back. My sister and I had given him a beer cooler that also went under the hull but survived intact. Backwash from the houseboat beaching pulled it out and it floated away down the river.

Mr and Mrs Ellis didn't stay at 'the spot' that night. They only stayed an hour and only because it took that long to get the houseboat off the beach. All of us pushed, apart from Mrs Ellis who sat at the controls powering the engines in full reverse, and my father, who had stormed off into the outback after a heated exchange. He'd demanded his mud-map back, which turned into a bit of jostling. Mrs Ellis tried to intervene and my father called her a whore. Someone also threw an onion but I can't remember who.

The spot's location was top secret after that. It didn't matter that my school friends had no idea where we were or how to get there, the turnoff blindfold was obligatory.

"Right, Peter, put on this blindfold."
"What?"
"David, help him put it on and make sure it's tight. I don't want him being able to see out of any gaps."
"Why do I have to put on a blindfold? What are you going to do to me?"
"We're not going to do anything to you, Peter. Just put on the fucking blindfold."
"I want to go home."

My father ended up going around to Mr and Mr's Ellis' house and apologising a few days later. He took them a bottle of wine and a Target gift voucher for $25 to go towards replacing a shirt that had been torn in the scuffle. They must have accepted his apology as they continued to play doubles matches together for years after until my father and Mrs Ellis had an affair and ran off together.

I was eleven the last time I went to the spot with my father. It was the weekend before he left. It was a good trip; usually my father was stingy about the amount of fuel the speedboat used but we spent all Saturday and Sunday on the water. He even let me drive the speedboat for a few minutes and later that evening, after the others had gone to bed, he poured some of his beer into a cup and let me have it. It was a still, dark night, there was no moon or breeze, and the water was like a black mirror. Stars reflected in it, making the cliffs look like they were floating in space. On our last night at the spot, my father and I sat by the river drinking beer.

My mother moved to a smaller house eleven years later and a lot of junk somehow ended up being stored at my place. I was in my final year at uni and living in a share-house with two other students; the garage wasn't being used to park in so it became everyone's catch-all place for 'stuff'. For two weeks, a pair of chickens lived in there after one of my housemates, Cynthia the vegan stick-insect, rescued them from a cage on the back of a truck. They got out one day when I opened the roller-door. Our share-house faced a busy main road and, as if choosing death over one more day in the garage, Douglas and Katherine ran straight into traffic. Douglas, which was a stupid name as chickens are girls, made it the furthest. Katherine went under a wheel in a flurry of feathers almost immediately but Douglas made it across the median strip and almost two lanes. If she hadn't looked back to check on Katherine, she'd have made it. I had to kick a hole in the garage wall, then chip away at the edges with a screwdriver, to make it look as if Douglas and Katherine had pecked their way out. Cynthia the vegan stick-insect never guessed otherwise.* She wanted to give them a burial but Douglas and Katherine were spread out over hundreds of feet and nobody was willing to stand in the road and halt traffic while she scraped them up.

---

* *Cynthia, if you are reading this, I really did feel bad. I'd grown quite attached to Douglas and when you weren't there, I'd let her inside to wander about a bit. She liked pizza crusts and Froot-Loops. Also, Geoffrey got her stoned once. I told him it was animal cruelty but he wouldn't listen. Really, he's the person you should be cross at.*

My friend Geoffrey was over one night. We were both antisocial so tended to be antisocial together often and were playing *Quake* that evening. For those unfamiliar with *Quake*, it's a game where you run around making grunting noises while being shot at. That's all there is to it. The game kept dropping the host and it was determined that the fault lay with an un-terminated ethernet cable. This was before the days of wi-fi, when everything had to be connected, and I had a box full of tangled cables in the garage somewhere.

"What does it look like?"
"It's cardboard, beige, and has four sides and a bottom. Kind of box shaped."
"There are hundreds of boxes in here, what is all this stuff?"
"Junk."
"Ooh! An Amiga 500. With a twenty-meg hard drive."
"It's yours if you want it."
"What would I do with an Amiga 500?"
"I don't know. You said 'ooh'."
"That's just an exclamation of surprise. Or more of a 'oh, what's this?' kind of thing. What's in this big canvas bag?"
"A tent."
"Ooh! What kind of tent?"
"Just a tent. My family used to go camping a lot. We owned a spot on the river. It was pretty nice."
"Do you still own it?"
"No... I don't know actually. Maybe. I haven't been there in over ten years."
"We should go camping."

"What for?"

"Because it's adventurous."

"Not really. Besides, there's more to camping than having a tent, you need sleeping bags and cooking utensils and stuff."

"My nephews have sleeping bags, they're in the cub scouts. I could borrow theirs. Come on, let's go this weekend. I've never been camping."

"What, ever?"

"I had a sleepover in a tent at a friend's house when I was a kid but that was just in his backyard. He was older than me and convinced me to play with his penis."

"Why do you tell me these things, Geoffrey?"

"It was his idea, not mine."

"Yes but why share personal information that's not relative?"

"You asked if I'd ever been camping."

"How much older was he?"

"I don't know, I was about ten so I guess he'd have been in his early thirties."

"Are you serious? That's not harmless exploration, that's molestation of a minor."

"No it's not, he didn't touch *my* penis. He just played with my hair while I touched his."

"Again, that's not really something that needs to be shared, except maybe with a counselor or the police. Why were you having a sleepover with an adult man?"

"Technically he was an adult but mentally, he was probably only eleven or twelve. He was in my under-twelve's gymnastics team so probably eleven."

"Right, so what you're telling me is that you want to go

camping because your only experience with the great outdoors is tossing off a mentally disabled thirty-year-old gymnast while he played with your hair in a tent."

"No, I want to go camping because I think it will be fun. And I didn't toss him off, I just squeezed and shook it a little bit."

"For how long?"

"Less than ten minutes."

"Oh, well that's fine then. As long as it was less than ten minutes of squeezing, shaking, and hair playing it really doesn't count. Did you cuddle afterwards?"

"No, we played Uno. Can we go camping?"

"There'd be no penis shaking or hair playing involved. I wouldn't want you to be bored. Besides, I was planning to work on my dissertation for Design History this weekend."

"When's it due?"

"Three weeks."

"That's plenty of time."

"It *is* meant to be nice weather this weekend..."

"Awesome. I'm going to take my mediaeval society armour and role play that we're weary knights on a quest, stopping to rest around a fire for the night to exchange stories and eat meat on a stick. I'll bring an extra chainmail vest and a chapeau à bec for you to wear. And a weapon."

"Right, I'm definitely not going now."

"Oh come on. You enjoyed the last mediaeval society event."

"I sat in the car while you all ran around whacking each other with swords."

"Fine, I won't take it."

Geoffrey did take his armour. It was in a 70's brown vinyl suitcase onto which Geoffrey had hand-painted a crest. The crest featured a knight's helmet above crossed swords dividing a shield into four sections. Each of these sections contained a different animal.

"You said you weren't going to bring your mediaeval stuff."
"It's better to have it and not need it than to need it and not have it."
"In what situation would you ever need chainmail while camping?"
"Bear attack."
"Yes, koalas can be pretty vicious."
"Koalas aren't bears. They're marsupials."
"They're the closest thing we have to bears in Australia."
"Fine, dingo attack then."
"Dingoes won't come anywhere near people."
"One stole a baby."
"That didn't happen. The mother killed and buried the baby and just said that a dingo took it."
"You're just saying that because she was a Seventh-day Adventist."
"She was tried and found guilty. Her religion has nothing to with it. I'm not even sure what a Seventh-day Adventist is."
"They're the ones that have sex through a hole in a sheet."
"They do? Why?"
"I don't know. So they can't see each other I suppose."
"Fair enough. I can see where that would be useful. You wouldn't have to bother doing your hair and the one under

the sheet could have a quick nap if they're bored. I'm assuming the woman lies under the sheet?"

"They probably mix it up a bit, take it in turns. Actually, now that I think about it, it might be Jews that have sex through a hole in a sheet."

"That makes more sense. Mark Shapiro* is a Jew and nobody would want to look at his fat head bobbing up and down above you while he's going to town. What's a Seventh-day Adventist then?"

"I'm not sure. Maybe they're the ones that believe an alien civilization lives on Haley's Comet and is going to pick them up the next time it passes."

"No, that's the Scientologists."

"Who knows then. They're all stupid. I'd give the sheet thing a go though."

"As your only interaction with the opposite sex is at your mediaeval society events, the sheet would be a necessity."

"What's that supposed to mean?"

"Who's that huge heifer with the moustache?"

I added Mark's name in here instead of the actual person because you have no idea who I'm talking about either way and I'm annoyed at Mark because he thinks rainbows come out of Trump's arse. Mark's chubbed up a bit since he started dating his new girlfriend, Emily. Emily says she's a chef but I'm not sure operating the waffle-press at iHop qualifies her as such. Come to think of it, Mark says he's Jewish but I've never seen one of those candle things or a wooden top at his house. I did see a huge turd in the toilet during a party at his place once though. It was about the size of a cat. I'm not sure if it was his or Emily's. Next time I visit, I'm going to check his sheets for holes. Probably with a pair of tongs.

"Louise? She's one of our best fighters."

"Only because she has so much momentum behind her. You'd need a fitted Californian king. What are the animals on your crest for?"

"What? Oh, they symbolise different things."

"Like what?"

"I'm not going to tell you because you'll only criticise."

"No I won't, I promise. What's the seagull for?"

"It's a swallow, it means 'bringer of good news.'"

"What kind of good news? Mediaeval society event cancellations?"

"News of the battle or a royal wedding. That kind of thing, normal mediaeval news. Maybe an occasional sonnet."

"Right, and the elephant?"

"It represents great strength."

"Ha, okay."

"See, I knew you'd criticise."

"I'm not criticising. What about the pig?"

"It's a boar. It symbolises standing your ground and fighting to the death."

"Unless Louise is running at you from behind a tree, screaming and waving about her wooden stick."

"It's a lance. A formidable weapon in the right hands."

"What about the turtle?"

"The *tortoise* symbolises invulnerability to attack."

"You cried when Douglas the chicken chased you through the kitchen."

"I didn't cry, dickhead. They were tears of rage. If I'd been wearing chainmail I wouldn't have even flinched."

We stopped in Morgan to get supplies. I bought ice for the cooler and enough food for two nights, Geoffrey bought an ice-cream and inflatable raft from the ice-cream and inflatable raft shop. The drive from Adelaide had taken over two hours. On the way, Geoffrey had wanted to stop in a small town named Truro to have lunch and take photos. It was the site of several murders in the late seventies and apparently he was related to one of the murderers.

"It's hardly a claim to fame, Geoffrey."
"Wow, jealous much? Sorry you're not related to anyone famous."
"Rolf Harris is my uncle."
"The wobbleboard guy? What a joke."*
"He's more famous than your murdering second cousin. Rolf Harris was in the British Paint's commercial. He tapped on the can and said, 'Trust British Paints? Sure can.' Everyone knows the slogan."
"It's weak. It's not even a slogan. It's just a question with a 'yes'. Trust pants? Sure, why not? Trust that cat over there? Probably."
"It's better than 'Let's bury the bodies at the Wingfield Dump.'"
"Not by much."

---

* *Interestingly, Geoffrey was a lot more impressed that I was related to Rolf Harris when Rolf was later charged with touching kids and went to jail for a few years than he ever was by Rolf's wobbleboard or paint can performances.*

It had been a long time since I'd been to the spot and my father had always driven. I knew the way, mostly, but only by landmarks. We exited Morgan and turned left at the post office, drove for almost thirty miles. Occasionally the river was visible and Geoffrey excitedly pointed it out each time.

"River!"
"Yes, I know Geoffrey. This road follows the river down so you're bound to catch glimpses."
"How long before... river!.. we get to the spot?"
"Another few miles before the turnoff, I'm meant to pull over at a big red rock somewhere up here and make you wear a blindfold before we go any further."
"What for?"
"So you don't know where the turnoff is. It was a thing my father made my friends do when I was young. So they wouldn't be able to disclose the location later."
"That's kind of creepy."
"Yes, one of my friends jumped out of the car while it was moving and ran."
"Did he get away?"
"To where? There's nothing out here. My father was pretty quick in those days, he played a lot of tennis. Even though he had to stop the car and get out, he still managed to tackle the kid in under fifty metres."
"We should totally do the blindfold thing though. River!"
"Why? Who are you going to tell?"
"That's not the point. If it's something you used to do, we should do it now."

"I don't have a blindfold."

"I can empty out of this Burger King bag and put that over my head."

"Go on then. At least it will stop you yelling out 'river' every thirty seconds."

"Please, even I'd get bored of saying it if it was every thirty seconds. I'll wait until we get to the big red rock. Otherwise people driving past will see me."

"Nobody has driven past the entire time we've been on this road."

"We're probably due then. I have to wait until we get to the big red rock anyway, it's tradition. Is that it?'"

"No."

"Is that it?"

No."

"River!"

We pulled over at the big red rock, it wasn't as big as I remembered, but it was still pretty big. Geoffrey stood on it and made me take a photo because it had been a theme since a previous trip away together. I then posed for a photo and did an action 'jumping off the rock' shot. It was easier to do it than argue. Geoffrey emptied out the Burger King bag and put it over his head as we pulled out and headed for the turnoff. It was the very next turnoff after the big red rock but the trick was to drive slowly to make it seem like it was further. I turned down the dirt road, which eventually split into two smaller paths, and I took the right. The path was poorly maintained, there were ruts and washed out areas and lots of overgrowth. I drove slowly but it was very bumpy and Geoffrey's bagged head bobbed and wobbled as if he was on a roller coaster."

"Can I take this off now? It's very disorientating."
"That's the point. You're meant to leave it on until we reach the first cattle gate but you can take it off anytime you want."
"No, I'll wait. How far away is the first cattle gate?"
"About five miles."
"Fuck that then," Geoffrey took off the bag and looked around, "river!"

We passed through the first cattle gate. There wasn't much left of it. A wooden fence post that once held the gate up had collapsed and the gate was somewhere in the overgrowth, pushed out of the way years before. The barbed-wire fence was completely down and nowhere to be seen. The second gate had always been down and the third was chained and padlocked.

"I forgot all about the padlock."
"Do you have the key?"
"Why would I have the key?"
"Oh no, what are we going to do? Can we walk to the spot from here?"
"No, it's still a few miles from here and I'm not carrying everything that far. The tent weighs a ton."
"We could try crashing through with the car."
"Sure, and then we can go over a big jump and freeze mid-

air while a voice-over asks, 'What have those Duke boys gotten themselves into now?'"
"The posts don't look very solid, maybe just try pushing one with the car to see if it'll break."
"That's not actually a terrible idea."

It was a terrible idea. I nudged the car slowly forwards until the pole was touching, then revved the engine. The pole held, I revved harder. My wheels slid in the dirt for a moment and then the pole suddenly gave out. Still revving hard, the car jumped forward, over the pole. The barbed wire fence, attached to the pole, wrapped itself around my front left tire, puncturing it with a fairly loud pop. I reversed the car several feet and we got out to survey the damage.

"This isn't a good start to the holiday."
"It's not a holiday, Geoffrey. It's a camping trip. Help me change the tire, there's a spare in the back."
"Do you want me to hold the lug nuts in the hubcap?"
"No, I want you to look for a flat rock or piece of wood to put under the jack, it won't be steady on loose dirt."
"Clever. You're like a professional tire changer."
"It's pretty standard procedure. It's written on the jack. You've never had a flat tire before?"
"Yes, but I called my dad and he came and changed it."
"Well we don't have that luxury out here. How's that flat rock or piece of wood search coming along?"
"I'm looking... Ooh, the fence is completely down over here behind this tree, we could have just driven around the gate."

The tree had been utilised as a fence post and as it grew over the years, the fence wire stretched and eventually gave way. We cleared the area of any remaining barbed wire, changed the tire, and detoured through the gap. After a few miles of bumps, ruts and a quick photo-op at a dead cow, the river came into view. I pulled up in a clearing beside the edge of the water and we both got out of the car.

The dock that my father had built was gone, washed away in a flood I suppose, and a fallen branch had demolished the shed he'd built, but apart from years of neglect, the spot was exactly the same as I remembered. Tall gum trees shaded two flat spots - one that we always pitched our tent on and another that I'd spent a morning with a pickaxe leveling - and a ring of rocks by the river's edge still showed evidence of years of camp fires. There were even a few beer cans among the grey ashes, faded well beyond determining if they were the same brand my father had preferred though. The afternoon sun was already lighting up the cliffs red on the far side of the river and a couple of pelicans swam slowly past, heading towards a giant weeping willow on the bank. The willow's roots twisted from the water and up onto the bank, creating a natural bench. Geoffrey stood on it with his hands on his hips, surveying the land like an English property baron.

"I thought it would be a lot bigger."
"It's ten acres."
"Yes, but that includes all the bits not on the river. Nobody

cares about those bits. I mean the campsite bit. And the river. Should we put up the tent?"

"Not yet. It's customary to sit by the river and have a beer before we do any work."

I drove back to the cattle gate to get the cooler. It had been taken out to gain access to the spare tire and set aside. Two folding chairs were leaning against it. I'd specifically asked Geoffrey if he had put everything back and he told me he had. When I commented such, after discovering the cooler was missing, he said, "I thought you meant the flat bit of wood for the jack."

I'd instructed Geoffrey to collect firewood while I was gone. When I returned to camp, he was wearing his chainmail and hacking at a piece of wood with a sword.

"Dost thou have refreshments my good fellow? My throat is parched and my bones weary from many miles of travel."

"Fuck off, Geoffrey. I'm not putting up with two days of dosts and thous."

"Fine. I am pretty thirsty though. Collecting firewood is a lot harder than I thought."

I unfolded the chairs and placed them on the edge of the river, with the cooler between to act as a table. We'd forgotten to bring a bottle opener but Geoffrey popped the lids off two cold bottles of Sparkling Ale with his sword. He was fairly pleased about it and smiled and did a little head wobble as if to say, 'See? My sword did come in useful' as he drove the point into the ground dramatically near his chair. It didn't go in very deep and fell over so he found a rock and hammered it in a bit, then we sat by the edge of the river and drank beer. The two pelicans glided out from the hanging willow branches, passing close by. Geoffrey threw them hotdog buns and told me that if this was the middle ages, he'd catch one of them and construct a turning spit-roast over the fire out of branches and reeds. We had a second beer. It was quiet on the river, a kookaburra laughed in the distance and a flock of cockatoos flew overhead squawking. The distant sound of an outboard motor grew louder and a houseboat cruised past, heading down the river.

"We're meant to give them the finger and yell at them to fuck off."
"Why would we do that?"
"I've no idea. It's just something my father used to do."
"Seems a bit rude. They've got as much right to be on the river as we have."
"I know."
"We should do it anyway though."

An old lady wearing a pink hat waved enthusiastically, we gave her the finger and yelled at her to fuck off. She went inside and the houseboat sped up a bit and disappeared around the bend. We had a third beer then decided to set up camp. The tent bag was heavy so we both carried it over to the primary flat spot, kicked a few small branches away to clear the area, and opened the bag. It was full of books.

'Why didn't you check it before we left?"

"It's the tent bag. It's always been the tent bag. Why would I need to check if the tent bag had a tent in it?"

"In case someone put books in it instead. Where's the tent?"

"How the fuck would I know?"

"Wow. You've ruined the holiday, David."

"It's not a holiday, Geoffrey. It's a camping trip."

"Not anymore. We don't have a tent. It's just a trip. I was really excited about the tent."

"I know you were. I don't know what to tell you."

"What are we going to do?"

"Go home I guess."

"That's not happening. I haven't even used my inflatable raft yet… Hey… do we have any rope?"

"What for?"

"We could run rope across two trees and use the raft as a tarpaulin to make a tent. It would be rudimentary but it would be shelter. And, if we built the fire near the opening, it would keep bugs away. It would be just like camping in the middle ages."

"People in the middle ages didn't camp under inflatable plastic rafts with the characters from *Friends* on it."

"It was either that or *Barbie*. Do we have any rope or not?"

"No, but I know where we can get some."

It took Geoffrey an hour to blow up the inflatable raft. I refused to help because he made so much spit you could hear it bubbling inside the mouthpiece. He changed into board-shorts and paddled across the river. I watched from my chair as he reached the other side. It was steep but the roots of the gum tree that my father had tied a rope swing to many years before weaved their way down into the water, creating natural steps. Geoffrey pulled the raft up onto a root, balanced it, and made his way up. He stood looking up at the tree for a few minutes then started climbing. He made it all the way up to the branch the rope was tied to, edged his way out and began to untie it. A light breeze caught the raft far below him; it swayed back and forth for a few seconds before sliding gently into the water. The river's current wasn't strong but there was definitely a flow, the raft rotated a few times as it headed off. Geoffrey hadn't noticed so I yelled to him. He was a fair distance away but looked around, waved, and went back to the knot. The rope fell and Geoffrey made his way back down the tree. Gathering the rope up in a loop, he approached the roots to climb down. The raft was well over a hundred feet away, moving quickly now that it had neared the middle of the river. Geoffrey raised his hands and yelled something.

"What?"

"The raft is floating away!"

"I know. Swim out and get it!"

"What?"

"Swim after it!"

"I'm not swimming. I don't know what's in the water."

"You're going to have to swim all the way back if you don't get to it."

"Oh yeah."

Geoffrey lowered himself delicately off the roots into the water, his foot touched something and he jumped back out quickly.

"Is there anything in the river that will bite me?"

"No. Just turtles."

"Do turtles bite?"

"...No. You'd better hurry, the raft's moving pretty quickly."

"I should have worn my shoes."

"Yes, probably."

"Okay. I'm going in. I'm really not happy about this though."

"You'll be fine."

Geoffrey secured the loop of rope around his neck and lowered himself into the water with a few yells of terror. Pushing off, he swam breaststroke towards the raft, keeping his head high above water and looking around nervously. The rope bobbed around his face, obscuring his view and tangling, so he took it off and held one end in his teeth, letting it trail. A fish jumped out of the water a few feet from him, creating a decent splash. Geoffrey screamed and swam faster, the rope discarded. He hadn't gained any distance on the raft and after a few minutes of fear-driven furious dedication, gave up. When I saw that he was abandoning the raft, I yelled, "Swim!" in encouragement but apparently he thought I yelled, "Fin!" which is why he screamed again and hurtled towards the shore as if he was bodysurfing a wave. He was sobbing as he climbed up the bank. The raft floated around the bend and was gone from sight.

"Well that was a fucking waste of time."

"At least you got a turn on the raft."

"What are we going to do now?"

"Go home."

"No, we're not giving up after one small setback. We'll just have to sleep under the stars like they did in the middle ages."

"I thought you said they slept under tarpaulins."

"Some of them. Some of them didn't have tarpaulins. It was hard times. Besides, it's warm and the sky is clear. It'll be nice. We can sleep around the fire. Like knights."

"I'll probably just sleep in the car."

"No you won't. How is that camping together?"

"Laying down in the dirt on the edge of the river isn't really camping."

"Fine, you can sleep in a chair. I'm going to do it properly though."

"There are scorpions around here."

"Are there? I might sleep in a chair as well then. It means I can jump up quicker if we're attacked by dingoes anyway. You should probably make yourself a spear."

We had hotdogs without buns for dinner. Geoffrey had forgotten to re-tie the bag when he grabbed the snack for the pelicans and it was full of ants. We cooked the hotdogs on a stick over the fire, like they did in the middle ages, and they were pretty good. We'd collected enough firewood from the surrounding brush to last the night and even dragged over a big old mallee stump to throw on top after the fire had some decent coals. We sat by the roaring fire drinking beer and watching the cliffs turn from red to orange and pink, then grey as dusk set in. Geoffrey was in full mediaeval armour, his sword across his lap. I'd finally agreed to wear the chapeau à bec, which turned out to be a Robin Hood cap, after Geoffrey complained about group participation. It had cooled as the sun reached the horizon, both of us had our legs in the sleeping bags Geoffrey had borrowed from his nephews; they were children's sleeping bags and only came to our waists. Mine had Buzz Lightyear on it, Geoffrey's was just red with the Ferrari logo. Fish splashed as they fed by the willow and a large egret waded slowly out from the hanging branches. It froze for a moment, then stabbed the water with its long beak, it's prize flashing silver in the last light.

Have you ever done a poo and it was so wet that when you wiped, it was like sticking the paper in a bucket of water?"
"Jesus Christ, Geoffrey. I was enjoying the moment."
"Well excuse me. Just making conversation."
"And you picked your swampy arse as the topic?"
"Well what would you like to talk about?"
"What?"
"Pick a topic."
"We don't need a topic. You're at the river, Geoffrey, relax and enjoy it. Have another beer and talk about river things."
"Like what?"
"Well, when I was kid, I used to jump off those cliffs. We should swim across and do that tomorrow."

"That's not happening. I'm never going back in that water again. It's terrifying."
"You're not going to go swimming at all?"
"No. Something touched my leg out in the deep bit."
"Fine, suit yourself."
"I will."
"Alright."
"Well that wasn't a very good conversation. I'm going to whittle a spoon out of wood."

Geoffrey whittled his spoon and I watched the flames. We both drank a lot of beer. The topics of conversation ranged from ideal spoon depth to whether we'd have sex with a shemale if she looked like Sandra Bullock and we were marooned together on a tropical island. Beyond the light and crackling of the fire, it was pitch black and silent. I put my head back and looked up at the stars. They were the same stars that my father had pointed out and named to me; the Southern Cross, George and Mildred, the Sheep and the Shoe.

I jerked awake in my chair, confused where I was for a moment. It was still dark but there was a hint of dawn approaching. The fire had gone out some time during the night and I was shivering with cold. A wisp of smoke from the ashes indicated that there might still be coals so I achingly leant forward and poked at them with a stick. Geoffrey was nowhere to be seen. He was asleep in the car. With the ignition on auxiliary and the heater running.

"Can we push start it?"

"No, you can't push-start an automatic. I can't believe this, Geoffrey. What the fuck where you thinking?"

"I was cold. And uncomfortable."

"You left me to the cold and uncomfort. Couldn't you have at least put more wood on the fire before you fucked off to your climate-controlled luxury suite?"

"It was still going when I got in the car."

"How were you cold if the fire was still going?"

"I wasn't cold until I got in the car."

"What?"

"I heard a noise."

'What kind of noise?"

"A rustle."

"Is that what knight's in the middle ages did? Heard a rustle and jumped into the nearest automobile?"

"Knights took it in turns to keep watch. They didn't all sleep at the same time. That's how you get stabbed."

"It was probably just a bird."

"No, it was a big rustle. A dingo-sized rustle."

"Right, well it's probably best you sought safety then. I mean, if it *had* been a dingo, there's no point in both of us being torn apart or dragged off into the darkness."

I could see you perfectly out of the window, I had the headlights on. If a dingo attacked you, I would have honked the horn."

"You had the headlights on? Were you listening to the radio as well?"

"No. There's no reception out here so I listened to CDs."

The battery was almost dead; there was barely a click when I turned the ignition. Words were said and then apologised for. A chair was kicked into the water and then retrieved with a sword. We had a lengthy discussion about electrons moving quicker when heated and decided it couldn't hurt to remove the battery and place it near the fire for an hour or so to warm it up but we both knew it was a stretch. The tire wrench didn't fit the bolts holding the battery in place but we managed to pry the clamps off with Geoffrey's sword and set the battery a few feet from the fire pit. I stoked the coals and added a few sticks and the Burger King bag to get it going. Geoffrey cooked the last of the hotdogs over the fire as the sun rose and I boiled a mug of water on the coals to make coffee. I'd bought milk, sugar and a jar of instant coffee in Morgan but forgot to buy water so I used melted ice from the cooler. We tried the battery after a few hours, it was quite warm to the touch but apparently the electrons weren't excited enough to care.

"We're stranded in the Outback. Like those people you hear about on the news that drive out into the Outback unprepared and die and you think, what an idiot, but this time it's us."
"We're not stranded, Geoffrey. Worse case scenario, one of us has to walk out to the main road and hitchhike into Morgan to get a replacement battery."
"It's miles back to main road, you'll never make it."
"What makes you think I'd be the one going? You're the one who drained the battery."

"I don't know the way. I was blindfolded. What's the best case scenario?"

"Well, a boat might cruise past. If we waved them down, they might give us a lift to Morgan... or, if the boat's bigger than just a fishing dinghy with a two-stroke on the back, they might let us use their battery to jump start the car."

"That's definitely the better option. So we just wait?"

"We were planning to stay another night anyway and there's nothing else we can do. I'll probably go for a swim when it warms up a bit."

"No, don't."

"Why not?"

"It's like one of those horror movies where one of them goes swimming and gets pulled under and the other one stands on the bank calling out to them and then goes close to the water and looks down and something grabs him as well."

"Then stay away from the edge if I get pulled under."

"I'd still be out here all alone. How long do you think it will be before a boat goes by?"

"Who knows."

"Should I make an SOS out of rocks on the bank?"

"Sure."

Geoffrey ran out of rocks halfway through the first S so he made it into an arrow instead. He also made a flag to wave by tying the Ferrari sleeping bag to a long branch. We sat by the edge of the river and waited. If this was a movie, there'd be a montage here to show the passing of time; it would include Geoffrey performing a flag dance and throwing it into the air and almost catching it, spear-fishing with his sword in ankle deep water, a game of who can throw a stick closest to the cooler, and three and a half games of charades.

"I give up, Geoffrey"
"Oh, come on. You gave up on the other two. Play this one out."
"Fine. So it's a movie, two words, first word sounds like violin. I have no idea. Do the second word... second word sounds like... finger? No? Ring?"
"Mmhm."
"Okay, second word sounds like ring. Violin ring... I give up, what is it?"
"*The Lion King*. I get to go again."
"*The Lion King* is three words. And violin doesn't sound anything like lion."
"It does if you mumble it."
"Right, I'm not playing anymore."
"Come on, one more go."
"No, it's just painful. I'm going to have another beer and then go for a swim."
"One more while you're having your beer."
"Fine."
"Okay... um... oh, okay, I've got one..."
"Movie."
"Mmhm."
"Two words."
"Mmhm."
"Is it *Those Magnificent Men in Their Flying Machines*?"

We froze. Geoffrey's eyes opened wide and he raised a finger to his lips. The distant but unmistakable noise of an outboard motor grew louder. It was coming from down river and we both ran to the bank and craned our necks to look around the bend. Geoffrey grabbed his flag and began waving it madly as a houseboat came into view. "Help!" he screamed. I waved my arms and yelled, "Hey!" as "Help!" seemed more something you'd yell if you were drowning or being attacked by a dingo - a flat battery lends itself more to, "Excuse me, sorry to trouble you." It looked like there were several people at the front of the houseboat and they were all looking our way. I waved frantically and decided "Help!" was a viable option. The houseboat was directly across from us when I realised it wasn't people; it was the cast from *Friends*. Geoffrey's raft was propped up against a railing and the old lady wearing a pink hat was standing beside it. She gave us the finger as the houseboat passed by.

"What a bitch!"
"I saw that coming as soon as I noticed the pink hat."
"She stole my raft and left us to die."
"We're not going to die. Another boat will come past eventually. I'm going for a swim."
"I might go in too actually. I'm pretty sweaty from waving the flag."
"I thought you were terrified of river monsters pulling you under?"
"At least it would be quick. It's better than slowly starving to death out here."

We swam across to the other side. I did the thing where you scream and go under the water as if something's pulled you under but Geoffrey just glared and kept swimming. To the left of the swinging rope tree, cliffs ran straight into the water but I remembered all the best spots to climb up. There was an old rusty iron pipe that ran all the way from the top of the cliff into the water, which we used to pull ourselves up onto a large smooth boulder. Geoffrey tanned himself like a giant white lizard while I climbed up to a ledge, ten or so feet above, and jumped off. I tried to convince Geoffrey to have a go but he wasn't having any of that and quoted made-up statistics of how many people die jumping off things into water. I climbed back up and jumped off several times. There were higher ledges above me but I hadn't been able to reach them when I was younger. Or perhaps it had just seemed too dangerous to jump from that height and I had never tried. I grabbed onto the iron pipe and lifted myself up; it was a good five feet higher than the first ledge. I'd never been this far up the cliff and it offered a great view. There was another ledge so I made my way up to it. Then another. I looked down, there was no way I was going to jump from this height but I could see far up the river. I climbed another ledge and the area flattened out somewhat. Using the iron pipe as a kind of banister rail, I was able to walk up to the very top from that point. I heard Geoffrey shout, "What are you doing?" from below and I yelled back that I was almost at the top of the cliff and could see for miles. I waited for him to scramble up to join me and we continued to the top together.

"What was at the top?" Seb asked. He was seven and it was his first time at the spot. We were sitting by the edge of the river drinking beer. I'd poured a little bit in a cup for him and he was sipping at it, making a face.

"Orange trees," I answered, "Thousands of orange trees. The iron pipe is an irrigation pipe that supplies an orchard. We walked through the orchard, eating oranges, and after about twenty minutes, came to a house with a big red barn. An old man was inside the barn, fixing his tractor, and we asked if we could use his phone. He called a mechanic in Morgan for us, who piloted his boat down the river and gave us a jump-start. We left that afternoon and this is the first time I've been back since."

"Have I met Geoffrey?"

"When you were a bit younger. He was struck by lightning at a Medieval Society event a few years back. Apparently they were out in the woods - probably chasing each other with swords - and ran and huddled together under a tree when a thunderstorm rolled in. A few of them survived, those that weren't wearing chainmail I suppose, but Geoffrey didn't make it. The news did a follow-up interview with one of the survivors a week or so later and her face was just burnt puss - bandages hid most of it but when she talked you could see she had no gums."

"What are you meant to do?"

"Sorry?"

"In a thunderstorm. Are you meant to just stand out in the open? That seems just as dangerous."

"I think you're meant to just lay down flat, so you're not the highest point. I'm not sure though, seems like a strange thing to do - to just lie down on the ground in the open getting wet. I'd probably run under a tree."

"At least he got to see the spot. It's nice out here."

"It is. If I ever make enough money, I'll build a cabin out here. Over the water, with cantilevers."

"What's a cantilever?"

"It's a projecting girder fixed at only one end."

"I like it how it is. Can we swim over to the cliffs and jump off?"

"Sure, after I finish my beer."

The sound of an outboard motor in the distance grew louder and a houseboat cruised around the bend. Seb grinned at me and I nodded.

About the Author

David Thorne is the unsolicited repetition of vocalizations made by another person. In his profound form he is automatic and effortless, and is a subset of imitative behavior whereby sounds or actions are imitated without explicit awareness. David occurs in many cases of autism spectrum disorder and Tourette syndrome. He can be the result of left hemisphere damage - specifically, damage to the frontal lobe of the left hemisphere. David Thorne has also been linked to several other neurological conditions, such as dementia, and can be the result of aphasia, schizophrenia, catatonia, epilepsy, stroke, or head injury.

David Thorne can occur immediately or some time after. In delayed David Thorne, repeated words, phrases, or multiple sentences occur after a delay that can be anywhere from hours to years. Immediate David Thorne results from quick recall of information from the short-term memory and superficial linguistic processing. Immediate David Thorne can be indicative that a developmental disorder exists, but this is not necessarily the case.

Immediate David Thorne can be indicative that a developmental disorder exists, but this is not necessarily the case.